PARENTING ADHD WITH EMPATHY AND EFFECTIVENESS

A Comprehensive Guide for Nurturing Success with Proven Strategies and Mindful Techniques to Improve Emotional Regulation, Focus, and Self Control

By
Sierra Nice

© **Copyright 2023 - All rights reserved.**

The content contained within this book may not be reproduced, duplicated or transmitted without direct written permission from the author or the publisher.

Under no circumstances will any blame or legal responsibility be held against the publisher, or author, for any damages, reparation, or monetary loss due to the information contained within this book, either directly or indirectly.

Legal Notice:

This book is copyright protected. It is only for personal use. You cannot amend, distribute, sell, use, quote or paraphrase any part, or the content within this book, without the consent of the author or publisher.

Disclaimer Notice:

Please note the information contained within this document is for educational and entertainment purposes only. All effort has been executed to present accurate, up to date, reliable, complete information. No warranties of any kind are declared or implied. Readers acknowledge that the author is not engaged in the rendering of legal, financial, medical or professional advice. The content within this book has been derived from various sources. Please consult a licensed professional before attempting any techniques outlined in this book.

By reading this document, the reader agrees that under no circumstances is the author responsible for any losses, direct or indirect, that are incurred as a result of the use of the information contained within this document, including, but not limited to, errors, omissions, or inaccuracies.

Content

Introduction 1

Part 1: Unpacking ADHD 4

    Chapter 1: Understanding ADHD with Compassion 5

    Chapter 2: The ADHD Brain: Unleashing Its Potential 19

    Chapter 3: Mindful Parenting Techniques 33

Part 2: Empowering Your Child's Development 51

    Chapter 4: Embracing Emotional Regulation 52

    Chapter 5: Fostering Focus and Attention 71

    Chapter 6: Self-Control Strategies for Daily Life 87

    Chapter 7: Time Management and Organization 108

Part 3: Nurturing Success in School and Beyond 125

    Chapter 8: Academic Success 126

    Chapter 9: Building Positive Relationships 140

Conclusion 156

    References 160

Introduction

Did you know that the famous Leonardo Da Vinci had ADHD? Yes, he did! He had a hard time finishing projects he started, hardly stayed in a place, and wasn't organized, even as an adult. Despite these difficulties, he went on to be an inventor, master painter, sculptor, mathematician, scientist, engineer, and architect.

Moving on, John F. Kennedy, the 35th president of the United States of America, had symptoms of ADHD. From his early years, he had trouble concentrating on things and was a poor student. Yet, he rose to fame as President of America who fought for the cause of human rights and was accredited with the saying, "Ask not what your country can do for you- ask what you can do for your country".

There are a lot of other famous people who were diagnosed with ADHD. I guess what I'm driving at is: ADHD is not a death sentence. That child of yours with this disorder has a strong chance of being great in life. They can fulfill their dreams. They can be successful, and it doesn't have to be just academically. You only need to help them find a dream that matches their interests.

This book will serve as a guide to accomplishing that. It'll enlighten you on what ADHD is all about and how to maximize it for greatness. I know that it's hard to always try to be there for your kid(s). They can't seem to do much for themselves and are causing a bit of trouble here and there.

At this point, all you may be thinking about is the "now" and how you can find solutions for them now. That alone can be burdensome, and I

Parenting ADHD with Empathy And Effectiveness

completely understand how you feel. I understand the weight you carry but cannot share it because you really love that child and will do anything to help them get on every day.

I know that you'd make sacrifices for them without a word of complaint, and always encourage them, even when you feel discouraged. I know you have tried to keep an eye on your teen with ADHD, but it seems like the more you try, the farther from you they get.

You see, one of my close cousins has ADHD. I know how his parents try to ensure he stays out of trouble. It was hard when he was growing up because they had to keep a close watch on him. One day, he almost got lost at the park because something caught his attention, and he just followed it on and on. We were lucky to find him that day.

As an adolescent now, he causes a lot of trouble from time to time. He even made a few attempts at suicide. Sometimes his parents would call me to find out what he had done this time and why the school was calling. They try their best, but then it still hurts their hearts.

So I spent time doing in-depth research on ADHD, and now I spend my time educating them on how to help their boy convert the energy for trouble into doing profitable things. I also spend time with my cousin to enlighten him on how to use his inattention and hyperactivity for good. Sometimes I dare him or set a challenge for him with a price he can't refuse. Today, he hasn't completely changed, but there are less and less calls from his school.

I can't promise you that when you read this book, you'll find a cure to your child's disorder (that's because there's no known cure yet), but I can promise you that parenting your ADHD child will get a whole lot better. You can consider this book a companion to alleviate the stress that comes with parenting your ADHD child.

In this book, you'll not only have a deeper understanding of ADHD, you'll also find practical solutions you can apply every day to make parenting easier. Now, I know all you think of is your child, but the solutions embedded in this book are not only for your child but also for you.

Introduction

You'll discover steps you can take to relieve stress and anxiety. You'll learn how to relate to your ADHD child in ways that will draw them closer to you. That way, you can be rest assured that you'll be their first dial/confidant.

By following the parenting techniques discussed in this book, you'll catch a glimpse of your child's possibilities. You'll see what your child can be and how to get them there. This book is rich with information that can change your parenting life for the better.

However, as you read, take note of the steps you need to take and the practical aspects, and apply them. It's through the application of these steps that you'll get the results you seek.

This book is for you if you have an ADHD child, or you have one who is related to one, or connected to you one way or another. It's also for you if you have an ADHD friend or colleague, or even if you're just a regular parent to regular kids.

And if you don't fall under any of the above categories, it's also for you because ADHD kids exist around you; if you've not met any yet, you may run into one someday. If and when you do, you'd want to be able to identify the condition and know how best to handle it. You don't want to be judgmental because you can't understand why a kid will behave so differently. But when you have first-hand knowledge about the condition , you'll be more welcoming, and this will earn you a bonus point before their parents and everyone else, that's amongst other benefits.

As they say, knowledge is power. The principles in this book will help you relate better to ADHD kids. Equip yourself with the right knowledge today about ADHD and share this knowledge with those who don't know about it and are struggling with ADHD kids. You can even recommend this book to them.

We're all trying to help make the world a better place, and this is my little contribution to the course. I hope you find all the answers you seek and help that child with ADHD become a better person future. Happy reading.

Part 1

Unpacking ADHD

Everything has a beginning, and beginnings are a reflection of what is to come. This is true of Attention Deficit Hyperactivity Disorder (ADHD). Understanding the nature of ADHD and the towering challenges attached to having a child with ADHD will prepare you for the beauty and the thorns of this disorder.

Get ready for a bumpy ride where your perspectives about ADHD will be poked and you'll be empowered with insightful facts to transform your relationship with an ADHD child and bring out the best in them.

Chapter 1

Understanding ADHD with Compassion

ADHD isn't a bad thing, it's a different way of thinking.
- **David Neeleman**

Defining ADHD: Beyond Labels

This is what a normal day looks like for an ADHD kid: Kayla, a seventh grader is our model. Kayla is a smart kid but has difficulties focusing on one thing at a time. Her biggest challenges are self-control and hyperactivity. On a normal day, Kayla finds it difficult to sleep, hence, waking up is always a challenge because no matter how loud and long her alarm blares she doesn't come to full consciousness.

Preparing for school is a tough one always for her parents. While in the lab at school, Kayla is fascinated with the procedures in the experiments, but she can't remember the second and third steps when she was asked to replicate what they were shown. During a Maths test, instead of focusing on solving the problems, she begins to worry about the possibility of failing and how her parents would feel about her.

This goes on and on every day. It's like a cycle they can break from. And instead of getting better, they are stuck. Going in a cycle or getting stuck for an ADHD kid is a big deal, hence the more reason they need parental interventions. Children are said to be gifts because of the happiness they bring to the family; however, after the joy of conception, there is a probability that after childbirth, there may be pain in the hearts of the parents due to complications or deformities in the child. This happens from time to time, and one such disorder that a child can be born with is Attention Deficit Hyperactivity Disorder (ADHD).

Parenting ADHD with Empathy And Effectiveness

Attention Deficit Hyperactivity Disorder (ADHD) refers to a condition that instigates restlessness, hyperactivity, and impulsiveness in a child with the disorder. This condition can be detected in children from age 6+.

ADHD is of three types:

1. **Predominantly Inattentive Disorder**: A child with this disorder finds it very difficult paying attention to something or someone. They can't listen to a conversation to the end because they either get lost somewhere in the middle or just drift off because of lost interest and find it boring. They make obvious mistakes. They are forgetful and disorganized. They misplace things easily and can't remember where they ever placed them. They avoid difficult tasks and when they are given assignments, they can't stay focused enough to finish in time. Sometimes, they even forget completely. They also find it difficult to remember instructions.

2. **Predominantly Hyperactive/Impulsive:** A child with this disorder is always on the move. Both their legs, minds, and mouths can't stay in one place for long. They're always talking, walking, running, and not paying attention. They can't wait their turn in class or in a queue. They act based on impulse. They don't think about the consequences of their actions on themselves or others, not even their friends. They can't control their emotions and burst out in anger without thinking of how the other person feels once they feel emotional discomfort.

3. **Combined type:** As the name implies, this is a merge of the two above types. This is when the child is hyperactive, impulsive, and inattentive. They combine all symptoms of lack of concentration, emotional instability, forgetfulness, and constant fidgeting.

Each stage has its peculiarity and ways of handling it. Moving on, the causes of ADHD are not specific, but there are medical conjectures about it such as complications at birth, genetics, alcohol or substance intake during pregnancy, premature birth, abnormal weight loss at birth, and extreme stress and anxiety during pregnancy.

Understanding ADHD with Compassion

Although scientists are still researching this subject, there's still no known cure for ADHD. According to research, about 10% of kids in America are diagnosed with ADHD, but only about 10% of them outgrow the disorder. For the others, it continues with reduced symptoms, or it stops for a while and returns. (Gillespie, 2023)

Therefore, once you notice its symptoms in your child, it's important to see a pediatrician who will analyze the type and severity of your child's condition. Once the severity is identified, the right therapy and treatment will then be prescribed.

ADHD is detected in boys earlier than girls because the symptoms in boys are mainly hyperactivity and impulsiveness. While it's true that boys love to play rough and do some crazy things even at a tender age, you will notice a different kind of rough with your boy child with ADHD. You may notice how he's always talking, even about irrelevant things, how he does dangerous stunts, or how he can't stay in a place. He's always on the move and will find it difficult to sleep.

The common symptom for girls, on the other hand, is inattention. This is not easily detected because you may think that your child is shy or an introvert. Or you may excuse it to be childish. However, as she grows older, say 12+, you may begin to notice the recurrent pattern of forgetfulness, or not paying attention to instructions, and you'll start getting complaints from her school.

Due to their abnormal behavior, people see ADHD children as unfit for society. That is not true. ADHD children are very special, with mind-blowing natural abilities and instincts. They are very creative, innovative, aspiring, friendly, kind, and they are bold communicators.

This is how they should be viewed. If you have a kid with ADHD, you'll notice how they quickly proffer solutions to problems and think outside the box. They freely express their opinions and say what's on their mind. You'll find out that as a parent, you can easily connect with them because they will tell you everything that goes on in their lives, even at school.

ADHD children are not to be seen as children with a disability but as children with unique natural abilities. Whatever disability they have cannot stop them from being even better than some normal kids if their abilities are harnessed and encouraged.

You need to pay special attention to what they can do, more than what they can't, and with the right amount of love, kind words, patience, and understanding, you will see how wonderful they will become. They will metamorphose from a burden to a blessing. It's all about your perspective.

As you read on, I want you to see ADHD children from the point of uniqueness with just a touch of peculiarity.

Breaking Stigmas: Navigating Societal Misconceptions

Society either fears or condemns what is different from the norm. They are used to the predictability, rationality, and precision of humans and they want things to remain like that. Once they see someone who has a different behavioral pattern, they tend to condemn and criticize, instead of getting to understand and appreciate it.

For this reason, a child with ADHD will likely be stigmatized by society. Children with ADHD are unpredictable and seen as dangerous by some people. At school, they will likely get bullied and mocked because of their behavior. In society, they may be discriminated against and looked down on as less.

Even parents of ADHD kids get it hard. They find it hard to associate with other people. They will always be self-conscious, especially when talking about or reprimanding other people's kids because they don't want to be insulted by their parents. They may not even have much time to socialize because they spend most of their time watching over their ADHD kids.

These can lead to low self-esteem in both parents and children, which will, in turn, make them live like outcasts. Such kids will prefer to stay in their shells at school so they don't get bullied or laughed at.

Understanding ADHD with Compassion

Nevertheless, this shouldn't stop them. As an adult (parents, teachers, elder siblings, relatives, etc,), the responsibility rests on you to ensure your child or such kids around you with ADHD, never miss out on the best life has to offer. You need to teach them more about their behavior, and how best to use it for good.

Instead of focusing on the negatives that come with it, teach them to focus on their positives. Instead of denying the condition and looking down on themselves, teach them to embrace it, expose them to the challenges that come with it, and also the many benefits that come with it.

You can organize a special meeting where anyone with such a challenge can come and talk about it. They can share their fears, challenges at home/school, and their peculiarities. Hearing others talk about a similar situation can go a long way in putting their young hearts to rest. It's a means of encouraging them.

You can also bring in adults with ADHD you know, who have successfully mastered their condition and have become better. If you don't know anyone, you can tell them stories or show them movies about people who are living with the condition but have made a name in society.

This will serve as a source of encouragement and build their resilience to dream big and pursue their dreams. It's all about creating the right mindset in them.

Furthermore, you can encourage their parents to attend these meetings. You can also teach them to research the condition. The more knowledge they have on the issue, the less worried both the parent and the child will be. The child will begin to see why he/she behaves the way they do and become conscious of it.

This will improve the way they see themselves and help them learn to live with their condition without having to let the negative comments of others get to them. After all, everyone needs one kind of motivation or the other.

Aside from that, you can also organize a lecture at school and for the community where you can enlighten other adults and other children about the condition. The more knowledge they have about it, the less likely they will condemn it. That's because they will begin to understand why these special kids don't behave like other normal kids.

At home, which is the heart of this matter, you need to shower ADHD kids with as much love as your heart can give. Now, note that you don't need to pity them. Don't try to do everything for them. Instead, treat them like you treat your other normal kids. Allow them to do things for themselves, and if you have to help, ask for their permission before you do.

At home also, never fail to speak kind words to them. Don't just flatter them with words, show them the beauty in themselves by pointing out their potential. If you can reprogram their mindset, it'll boost their confidence even when they are outside. They need to have a positive mindset about themselves.

If you're able to do this, coupled with the prescribed treatment, you won't just be helping your child, but other children with ADHD become better people in future.

Building a Supportive Network: Empowering Parents

At some point in your life, you've had to rely on someone for support. That's because no man is an island. We all need love and support, especially from those we call friends and family. Parents aren't left out.

You see, there is an unconscious preconceived notion that parents are strong, and are adults and therefore, should be able to take on anything. It's rare to see an adult cry. They're not permitted to be sad or mad or worried. It's like the mindset sets them to be immune to feelings or never express them publicly.

This has made parents pretend while dying within. Among parents, parents with ADHD children need all the support they can get. If you have a neighbor with an ADHD child who is always smiling, don't think they don't have feelings. Irrespective of how understanding and endearing a parent with such a child can be, there'll always be days when they're down.

It's important that, as a parent with such a child, or a concerned adult, you build a strong support network around you and your kid(s). A support network is a steady source of motivation, resources, and encouragement.

Your support network can be your friends, family, relatives, neighbors, and other professionals, like your doctor/pediatrician, or teachers, at your kid's school. They are there to encourage you when you're down, and also help you out financially or materially. They are like the pillars you rest on when you're tired.

Your support network helps you deal with stress and anxiety and its related problems. You'll feel better as a parent when you can talk freely in your child's PTA meeting without eyebrows being raised at you. You'll feel relieved when you see your kid with ADHD playing gleefully with your neighbors kids.

As a parent with such a child, you'll feel relieved when you have time for yourself because your parents have come to take their grandkids on holiday. With all these support systems around you, you will feel a lot better. This will enable you to develop a positive mindset and give your ADHD kid (s) all the love and support they need. That's because you have a steady source of it.

Otherwise, you can't give what you don't have. If you don't have a support network at home, work, and the community where you live, your mind will always be clouded. No matter how hard you try to stay positive, you'll always hear or see something that will return you to your depressed state.

The result of this is that your ADHD kid will suffer for it because what they receive at home, whether positive or negative, will greatly determine how they'll see themselves, and how their lives will turn out. Even normal children who don't receive love at home tend to find it in the wrong association or turn to drugs and alcohol.

As a parent, you're your child's first support system. If you're not supported, you'll find it hard to support your special child. Another thing is that you have to be open enough to accept support from those who give it. If you refuse to accept support because of whatever reasons you give, you'll likely crash someday.

So, be open to receiving and even demanding support, as the case may be. Disassociate yourself from anyone who constantly talks down on your child because of his /her disorder, whether directly or indirectly. Surround yourself with a group of people who encourage you and see the best in your child.

In addition, you can join or create a group of other parents who have children with one deficiency or the other. Talking to other people and hearing their experiences will help relieve you. You'll no longer feel alone. You can make friends from such gatherings and share your feelings with them from time to time. If there are no physical groups available, you can connect with such groups online (Shakibaie, 2023).

Aside from that, you can also read stories and watch documentaries about people who had one defect or another who made it big in life. This will give you a positive mindset and make you see your child, not for what they are today, but all they can be.

As you go on, always be truthful to yourself. Understand your feelings and don't be ashamed to accept them. It's better to pour out your feelings to a friend, than bottle it up. One day, it may decide to flow and it definitely will not end well.

Self-Compassion for Parents: The Foundation for Empathetic Parenting

While it's true that children with ADHD go through a lot of stress, their parents have it hard too. Parents with ADHD kids go through physical, emotional, and psychological stress. They have to give love, care, and attention to their kids and it can be draining.

Understanding ADHD with Compassion

It becomes more difficult when their child is self-destructive, which is one of the characteristics of children with ADHD. As a parent, it's hard when you're called to your kid's school to be informed that he/she tried jumping a fence, or harmed themselves during a science experiment.

This can lead to frustration and depression. It gets worse when you're seen as incompetent by society and incapable of taking care of your child, whom you know you've done everything for. All these can stress you out and make you look older than your age. It can also affect your health.

That's why you need to engage in self-compassion. Self-compassion is the act of showing yourself compassion and care. It's self-love and looking out for yourself and your health. This is very important.

You see, you can't give so much love while receiving spite from people around you. At some point, you'll run out of love to give. You need a source of love, where you can be refreshed from time to time. That's why having a strong support network is important.

However, whether or not you have one, you need to show yourself some love. You need to make time for yourself. Take yourself out to a nice meal, or fix a spa day. Take time to listen to healthy podcasts and music. When you're alone, do things that will make you happy.

You can go swimming, watch good movies, dance, play a game, read a book. Whatever makes you feel relaxed. If you don't have a hobby, then you can develop one. If you have a spouse, you can do something that you both love from time to time.

It can be when the kids are at school, or you can send them to their grandparents during the holidays. Whatever you need to do to create time. It doesn't have to be every day, but you need that time for yourself.

In addition, you need to pay particular attention to your mind. Your mind is the engine house of your body. If your mindset is negative, your attitude will be negative too, and a negative mindset is easy to get in a case like this.

You need to fill your mind with positive information. You can adopt mindfulness meditation to help relieve you of stress. Allow yourself to live in the present and release your mind from hurtful statements, pain and anxiety.

When you hear negative comments from people around you, don't let it affect you. Build a healthy mindset and let their comments bounce off. You need to develop your mind to the point that it doesn't get affected by what people do or say.

You should never beat yourself up, or blame yourself for your child's condition. You shouldn't isolate yourself or look down on yourself because of your child's condition. You need to understand that you're not responsible for it, and you need to know that you can and should be happy.

ADHD in Different Age Groups: Understanding Developmental Nuances

Attention deficit hyperactivity disorder (ADHD) is mainly detected in childhood. It can be detected as early as 6 years, but it doesn't have a known cure, so it progresses into adolescence and adulthood. So, the myth that adults don't have ADHD is false.

The only difference is that the symptoms differ as the child grows. Each phase of their life has its own peculiarity and challenges. The prominent type of ADHD found in kids is the predominant hyperactivity. Kids with this disorder tend to be hyperactive. They are always fidgeting and unable to stay in a place. At school, they are always talking and interrupting the teachers or their peers.

This is not preplanned. They don't even know why they can't keep calm. They can't stay at a place to finish an assignment, or successfully carry out a given task at school. This makes succeeding academically very hard. However, the hyperactivity reduces as they grow.

As they grow into adolescents, their hyperactivity reduces but their impulsiveness increases. This is a more dangerous stage because aside from the disorder, they also are at that stage in their lives where they are seeking to discover themselves. As a parent, you need to really monitor your child at this stage.

The impulsiveness caused by the disorder can make them do dangerous and harmful things even to themselves without thinking it through. If not properly checked, they can get negatively influenced by the taunts of their peers and relapse to alcohol or riotous living just to survive.

However, as they grow into adults, their hyperactivity and impulsive nature reduces, and their inattentive nature increases. As adults, they'd find it difficult to concentrate at work or at home. They are lost during a conversation and seem to pay close attention to anything for long.

It's difficult for such adults to be productive in their workplace because they're not focused or organized. They can't organize their desks at work, or rooms at home, and they are forgetful. It's like no information can stay in their brain for up to a day (Kumperscak, 2013).

This can cause lapses in their finances, relationships, sexual lives, office life, and their health too. They seem like big babies because they still need someone to keep them in check if they'd do anything productive with their lives.

So saying, you can see that children with ADHD undergo developmental changes as they grow. But the bottom line is that they always need love, care, and help from those around them.

Recognizing Co-Existing Conditions

One thing about ADHD is that it doesn't come alone. It comes with various other issues that complicate the life of the patient. It's important you know these coexisting conditions, so you can easily identify them, and find solutions.

- **Conduct disorder:** This is common in teenagers, especially those who combine hyperactivity and impulsiveness. They are unable to control their emotions once there is a trigger. They can't control their temper and they become hostile towards others. They can break rules and not care about the consequences. When they get like this, it's hard to calm them down till they've done all their impulse tells them to do. This can be very dangerous because they can go into substance abuse or even stab someone, or do something crazier. At this point, they're out of control.

- **Learning disability:** ADHD triggers learning disabilities, but it promotes it. People with ADHD can't focus on learning. They are either too uneasy to sit at a place and learn, or they're just indifferent about it. Whatever the case may be, they can't learn, and if they can't learn, then they can't be productive academically.

- **Bipolar disorder:** This is a type of disorder that leads to depression. It's a mood depression otherwise called Oppositional defiant disorder (ODD). People with ADHD are always feeling down and seeing the worst in themselves. This feeling intensifies at adolescence, and it can lead the patient to commit suicide or take on other illegal or irresponsible activities in order to feel relief.

- **Anxiety disorder:** People with ADHD tend to always be unnecessarily worried. Their minds are always busy worrying over something that happened, or that hasn't even happened. They can't seem to find peace within themselves as their mind is always in turmoil.

- **Autism spectrum disorders:** ASD is a disorder that renders the patient incapable of communicating effectively, acting right, or learning things. It's a neurological disorder and it can hamper the productivity of the patient. It is diagnosed from age 2+. Aside from being unproductive, behaving strangely, acting out of context, and being overly sensitive, ASD can also lead to irritability and insomnia.

- **Tourette's syndrome:** TS causes irregular movement of the head or shoulder (twitches) while making loud sounds called tics. These sounds

Understanding ADHD with Compassion

can be very disturbing. It can be a shameful experience for kids because it just happens and they can't truly control when or where it happens. This syndrome is prevalent in kids with ADHD.

The key to living a better life is early detection. Once you notice any abnormality in your toddler or preschooler, go see a pediatrician. When it's detected early, treatment can be administered early.

Now, although the treatment will not completely take away ADHD, it will reduce its effects, and also contain the coexisting conditions.

The Genetic Component of ADHD

ADHD can be caused by several factors like premature birth, alcohol intake during pregnancy, or other complications at birth like epilepsy or brain damage. However, aside from these factors, ADHD is said to be passed genetically.

It means if parents have ADHD, there's an 80% possibility that one or two of their kids will be prone to having it too. There's a higher chance of kids having it from first-degree relatives than the public. The only thing that is unsure is the severity of it.

Research has continued to date about the primary genes responsible for the transfer of ADHD. Scientists suspect that the genes may be present in the dopaminergic neurotransmission system. They suspect the dopamine D4 and the dopamine D5 genes. Yet, it's still unsure due to the complex nature of the disorder.

Also, the disorder is linked to some deficiencies in some key parts of the brain that are responsible for retention, coordination and right thinking (Collingwood, 2016).

As research continues in this area, scientists hope to find the exact genes responsible and find a cure for this disorder or better ways of managing it.

Takeaway One

ADHD is a condition that is characterized by hyperactivity, impulsiveness, and inattention. There is no known cure for this disorder so it continues from childhood (when it's first detected), to adolescence, and then adulthood.

The characteristics of ADHD are individually prevalent at certain stages of life. In childhood, hyperactivity is prevalent. In adolescence, impulsiveness takes over while hyperactivity drops. Then in adulthood, hyperactivity and impulsiveness drop to a minimum, and inattention is prevalent.

So, if you have a kid, parents or colleague who has the disorder, you need to watch them closely so they don't do anything to hurt themselves. It's true they can be a handful, but they have the potential to make up for their inadequacies.

Chapter 2

The ADHD Brain: Unleashing Its Potential

Kids have a lot of gifts from their ADHD: Unending creativity, thinking outside the box, energy, enthusiasm and passion about their interests.
— C. J. Dr. Griffin

It might interest you to know that the renowned Virgin Group wasn't founded by a normal kid. It was a kid who couldn't focus on one thing at a time that channeled his energy into creating businesses under a single umbrella. Richard Branson, founder of Virgin Group, was diagnosed with ADHD, but he went on to succeed despite the disorder. He couldn't fit in at school, but he found a borderless sector to leverage the disorder and explore his creative strength. That's how he was able to build one of the world's largest enterprise.

When you think of ADHD, you think of how to tame it; but that's as good as destroying the kid who has it. Unleashing the potential of ADHD requires shattering stereotypes and borderless thinking. An ADHD child needs that much.

The ADHD Brain: Strengths and Challenges

Parenting an ADHD child can be quite challenging, not only because you can't predict their next move but also because they can't even control themselves. It's like they're being driven by a force inside their brain, and they just move as their mind instructs. That can be scary at times.

You see, a lot goes on in the brains of ADHD kids. But due to some deficiency in the performance of some core parts of the brain, like the prefrontal cortex, temporal and parietal cortex, etc., they find it hard to concentrate, stay still, be coordinated, or retain information.

All of these can pose a serious challenge for these kids. For one, it can lead to low self-esteem. That's because they may fall into the category of being bullied at school. Teachers will constantly be on their necks to finish an assignment, sit still in class, complete a drawing, or finish a school project. It will make them academically poor.

This, plus the fact that they will see that they don't act like other kids, will lead them to believe they are dull, weird, and odd. Low self-esteem will further lead to isolation. The fact that they can't help it worsens the case. They'd prefer to stay alone and not fight back. They will rather relapse into the world in their mind or a place where they feel safe. A place where they don't feel judged or looked down on for being different—a difference they weren't responsible for. This place can be a corner at school or their home if they feel loved there.

However, some other kids with ADHD will likely end up in the wrong group and go into drugs and alcohol to dull the pain they feel in their hearts. They would choose to become defiant toward bullies and teachers instead of succumbing to their negative comments.

Their hyperactive and impulsive nature can make them ticking bombs. They are not in control of their actions, so if not closely watched, they can commit suicide or hurt others and themselves unintentionally. This gets them in a lot of trouble most of the time.

On the other hand, their inattentive nature will make them disorganized, forgetful, and often oblivious to their surroundings. They can't focus on a conversation or try out difficult tasks; they would rather avoid every kind of social activity. They would lose friends, jobs (for adults), relationships, and vital opportunities.

All of these challenges and more are peculiar to kids with ADHD, and they continue even as they grow into adults. These challenges are real and can

The ADHD Brain: Unleashing Its Potential

be daunting. They're already a handful, and if they focus on them alone, they will end up doing nothing reasonable with their lives as an ADHD child.

However, according to the natural order of things, whatever has advantages also has disadvantages. Here, I'll say that ADHD has disadvantages and lots of useful advantages. These advantages are seen as the superpowers of ADHD kids because they are more common in them than in normal kids.

These advantages are a result of the neurodiversity of their brain. What is termed a deficiency can be a force for good. It's these advantages that make ADHD kids a blessing, and it's the sweetest part of parenting ADHD kids.

These advantages include:

- **Hyperactivity: Their** hyperactivity makes them always active, and they hardly get tired. While this is seen as a disadvantage at school, it can be a positive force in life. It means they will have more energy to carry out tasks than normal kids. If they choose to be athletes, they already have the natural ability to be active. So it's a plus.

- **Hyperfocus:** Hyperfocus is the ability to focus on a particular thing of interest for a long time. This is a disadvantage if seen from the perspective that they won't do well in other subjects at school. However, if seen from a positive perspective, it's a great advantage. It means if they find a sport, activity, or course that interests them, they can give it the best shot and become great at it. This will do them a lot of good as they choose a career path in life, because honestly, out of all we learn at school, we have to choose one thing to do.

- **Resilience:** Resilience is the ability to hold onto something irrespective of the difficulty. Kids with ADHD go through a lot of challenges both at home, at school, and in the community at large. This strengthens their will and resolve. They're able to withstand pressure and adapt to a chaotic change easily. With the right supportthey can channel this into whatever they choose to do in life. Once they do that, they can go through anything till they achieve that area of interest.

- **Creativity/Innovation:** A lot of ADHD kids are creative and innovative. That's because they have a lot going on in their mind at the same time. They have a vast imagination and can bring up brilliant ideas on how to do whatever interests them. When they focus on a thing of interest, where others see white and black, they see a spectrum of colors. This makes them stand out from their peers in activities that interest them. It also makes them great inventors and scientists.

- **Thinking outside the box:** One of the characteristics of ADHD kids is that they talk a lot and can't wait to continue talking although it's not a defining characteristic of ADHD. This implies that they can talk about a lot of different subjects, whether relevant or not, at the same time. This makes them great thinkers. They have the ability to think up ideas and solutions quickly.

- **Empathetic and kind:** Most kids with ADHD are empathetic and kind. That's because they don't have the ability to think logically and chronologically like others. If they see something, they immediately blurt out exactly what comes to their mind. They don't have the ability to think about how others feel. That's what makes them kind. They feel what others feel immediately. If they see someone crying, they don't think, they just go to the person and console the person. This makes them good friends.

- **Great communicators:** ADHD kids are prone to saying what is on their mind. They react and respond simultaneously. This makes them great communicators. They only need the right coaching. They are spontaneous and just do things as they come to them. This can be unhealthy, but also healthy in different other ways.

So, while parenting ADHD kids can be a handful, the right treatment, therapy, and amount of love from you, the parent, will go a long way in shaping these kids. It'll help them harness their innate abilities that seem like a disadvantage, and channel them into positive activities that'll be beneficial to them.

Therefore, as a parent, as you watch out for ways to help them overcome the challenges they face, don't also forget to find ways to boost their strengths so they can have something to fall back on.

Neurodiversity and Resilience

ADHD kids have a uniquely wired brain. It's unlike that of neurotypicals (normal kids). They lack the ability to concentrate on a task, initiate one (if they do, they can't stay on track for long), or feel content after carrying out one. That's because they have low dopamine levels.

Dopamine is a chemical in the brain that's responsible for making you feel satisfied or rewarded after carrying out a task. Without this, your executive functions are impaired. There'll be no motivation whatsoever to do anything, and trying to do anything without motivation takes extra effort, it's tiring and very boring.

This is responsible for the neurodiversity of the ADHD brain. Neurodiversity is the difference in their brain that is responsible for the way they act or respond to situations. Their neurodiverse brain is different from neurotypical brains. That's why they can't focus like others, or complete a task, take on difficult tasks, or stay still like neurotypicals.

The neurodiversity of their brains makes living normally difficult. Due to the fact that they don't act normally, other kids may tend to avoid them. It can also cause them to see themselves as weird and not fit in the society. However, if they can look beyond all that negative, they'll see the benefits to neurodiversity.

One main benefit is resilience. Resilience is the ability to stay on a difficult course and bounce back from a difficult situation without giving up. ADHD kids grow to be fighters and survivors. It's like doing one thing for years. You'll become a master at it.

Despite the spite, shame, disgrace, and bullying they go through in life, they never give up. The therapy that they're made to undergo also boosts their resilience. The therapy boosts their understanding and instils a positive mindset in them about their condition.

The encouragement and love they get at home from parents and relatives also helps. You may wonder why the therapy works well when it's easier for them to just stay in their shell. You may wonder why they choose to continue receiving hurtful statements and still go on. Well, it's simply because they are very open-minded. They feel everything around them that catches their interest, so it's easy to accept whatever their therapist tells them. They get hurt when they get bullied but get encouraged and ready to move out again like both happened once they are motivated.

As they push through school days, college, and their environment before they become adults, they will have mastered the art of resilience. At this point, they must have undergone a series of therapy sessions and had a level of control over themselves.

At this point, although they may still not be able to focus at work, you can be sure that they won't give up until they somehow accomplish their task. They no longer cower in shame or fear at negative comments. In fact, some ADHD kids/adults learn to accept their condition and focus on harnessing their innate potential. They spend more time on things they love and have an interest in, than on things that they can't focus on. As a parent, you should encourage your ADHD child to pursue what they love, even if it's not academics. With the right kind of motivation, they will excel.

Brain-Boosting Activities for Kids: Unlocking Cognitive Potential

Babies are a beauty to behold. They are so small and cute. Another part of a baby that is to be focused on is their mind. Their minds are like a blank sheet and very innocent. However, as your baby grows, they need you to give them things to fill their minds with. They can't grow with a plain mind.

The things you expose them to, will help build their cognitive abilities. Now, this process has to be done step-by-step, little by little. There are activities

The ADHD Brain: Unleashing Its Potential

that are necessary for each stage. These activities are simple but they serve a different function in helping your child's brain development.

At 0-6 months, you should be close to your baby. Always be there when they call for your attention. Carry them, feed them, talk and sing to them, dance slowly with them, and cuddle them more. The more you do this, the better your bond with them.

As they grow, play more with them. It can be from a simple peekaboo to hide and seek. Read stories to them and teach them rhymes and simple songs like Twinkle Twinkle Little Star, Happy Birthday, and other common songs.

When they have mastered their environment, you can play games with them and solve simple puzzles with them like peg puzzles, shape puzzles, etc. You can also teach them to play building blocks and physical games.

You can get them colors and teach them to draw or scribble things down. Get different toys that portray various careers, like a doctor, an engineer toy, or super heroes and Barbies.

One thing about kids is that they believe whatever you tell them, so you can make anything into a game. You can turn eating into an airplane game. You move the spoon in the air as if it's an airplane while making a speed sound and move it to their mouth. Teach them to do the same and put the spoon in your mouth or theirs.

You can teach them to pour water or milk (whatever they like) from one cup to another without spilling it. Take them to the park and encourage them to play with other kids. You can also let them choose the ice-cream they want from the ice-cream shop.

Now, all of these seem very simple, but they go a long way in developing the cognitive abilities of kids. These games develop their eye-hand and mind coordination, improve their social skills, their decision making ability, allow them to express themselves, improve their motor skills, and so much more.

Other things like cartoons and fantasy stories, like Alice in Wonderland, open their mind to a whole new world of imagination. They learn to laugh, be amazed, cry, feel sad, and feel overly happy as the story unfolds. You can also let them watch academic videos, like Dora the Explorer, and others that teach simple sentences, words and expressions via an adventure or song.

When they see and are able to identify an object on TV, it'll stick in their minds and they'll be able to identify it when they see it. I tell you, educational videos will go a long way in helping your kids than you think. It can even be educational games.

As your kids grow, know that they learn from you and what they see. If you're always cooking and singing, don't be surprised when you see your 3-year-old daughter pretending to cook for her dolls and singing. Again, as your kids grow, pay close attention to what they do, and what interests them.

When you expose them to lots of positive brain-boosting activities, it'll be easy for their innate potential to find expression. You may notice that when others are playing hide-and-seek, your little boy prefers to paint mum and dad. Or you may notice your baby girl is tending to her dolls, feeding them, and putting them to sleep.

When you notice certain traits in your kids, it's best to encourage them and help them develop it. It doesn't even have to be something physical. It can just be that you notice that one of your kids is more compassionate and kind than others.

They always want to share what they have with others, or they show care for someone who is sick. These are traits you should look out for and encourage.

The Role of Medication: Benefits, Concerns and Alternatives

When you get sick, you take drugs to get well. There are different kinds of drugs, designed to treat different kinds of problems. When ingested, drugs are capable of affecting our physical and mental state.

The ADHD Brain: Unleashing Its Potential

For an ADHD patient, medication is one of the treatments that can be employed to rectify the deficiencies that cause anomalies in the patient. Stimulants are usually prescribed for ADHD patients, and the result will be an improved ability to concentrate, think, and carry out tasks completely.

Don't be too optimistic to conclude that these medications are permanent remedies for ADHD because there are none as of now. However, they can help alleviate the effects of ADHD on kids. Besides, these medications can't work alone just as medications for other ailments are not wholistic. Doctors usually recommend some other activities, like physical exercise, eating certain meals, taking lots of water, etc. For ADHD, medication is just one of the alleviative treatments. It can work along with therapies and some other recommendations as you'll find in this book later.

Generally, drugs are like messengers. They carry out the message they were designed for. That's why it's important to get a prescription from a doctor after proper examination, before taking any drug. Taking the wrong drug to solve a problem will only cause more problems.

While medication is very good, it also has its side effects. You see, drugs are chemical substances, and chemical substances have their side effects on humans, some more serious than others.

For instance, some side effects of ADHD drugs are:

- Loss of appetite
- Trouble sleeping
- Stomach upset
- Tics
- Unstable blood and heart rate
- Increased anxiety
- Loss of weight

These side effects are not permanent, but they continue until the body gets used to the drugs. It's the same for almost all drugs. Some drugs have mild side effects like rashes, itching, dizziness, forgetfulness, and noise in the mind. However, some have more severe side effects like liver damage, high blood pressure, bleeding, etc.

Aside from the common side effects of ADHD medications, there are some rare, serious side effects of ADHD, like psychosis and heart problems. This is one of the reasons why self-medication isn't encouraged. Even if you know the name of the stimulants to use for your kid, you still need a doctor's prescription, because ADHD does not manifest in kids the same way. If your kid has another health condition, taking just any ADHD medication could worsen things for the kid.

This tells you the peculiarity of drugs. As helpful as they are, they come with rules and regulations. If you defy their rules, you'll suffer for it. You can't just take drugs because you'd taken it before for that same situation and it worked. That's drug abuse.

There are alternatives for medications, some of which will be robustly discussed later in this book. But suffice it to mention here that these alternatives require the active participation of both parents and kids. Alternatives like Cognitive Behavioral Therapy (CBT), psychoeducation, behavior therapy, parent training and education skills, etc., all require the involvement of parents. As you can see from the list, there are trainings you need to undertake to get the best out of your kid, just as this book is a resource designed to help you achieve the same result.

Therefore, it's not just an ADHD kid that needs help in this regard, even parents need it, hence the alternative for medications.

Dietary and Lifestyle Factors: Nutrition for Optimal Brain Health

Most times we are tempted to eat what we want at any time we feel like. Honestly, street food seems to get tastier every time you eat it, right? Then again, the quick snacks and morning cereals seem too important to let go of.

The ADHD Brain: Unleashing Its Potential

Well, all these may be true, but it's high time you looked at the bigger picture. Eating unhealthy meals and junk food does you more harm than good. Aside from the fact that they have no nutritional value, they cause problems for your body and your brain.

There is an ongoing body of research on the impact of diet on ADHD kids. There are certain meals that trigger hyperactivity and impulsivity in ADHD kids. You can guess which one—glucose of course! Perhaps you didn't know that allowing an ADHD kid to feed on junk and unhealthy meals isn't a demonstration of affection, but now I'm telling you that it's not. Living on those types of food increases their propensity to exhibit more characteristics of ADHD after the meal diffuses into their bloodstreams.

Generally, eating unhealthy meals like sugary foods and drinks can reduce the brain's ability to learn or retain information. It also causes irritation and anxiety, and excess sugar leads to other health issues like diabetes.

Other disadvantages of unhealthy meals include the inflammation of the hippocampus, which can lead to depression, and the inability to plan focus or think. They also activate stress hormones because the brain can't work with what it's getting. There are no sufficient nutrients to develop.

Allowing an ADHD kid to keep gulping down unhealthy meals and expecting them to be the best at work or what they do is like starving a child and expecting them to grow healthy and robust. That's impossible.

The link between diet and the brain cannot be broken. The brain needs healthy meals that provide the right nutrients in the right quantity for it to develop and function properly. It's like giving a carpenter all the tools he needs to build a dollhouse. He will complete it in no time.

Eating healthy meals increases the Brain-derived neurotrophic factor (BDNF). BDNF is a molecule used by neurons in the hippocampus, and it increases our cognitive abilities, increases neurogenesis (that is, the production of neurons in the brain), and protects neurons from dying.

Neurons are very important because they aid our ability to think, learn, retain, and communicate effectively. Without them, our cognitive abilities will be impaired. (Unhealthy meals limit the production of these neurons.)

Furthermore, healthy meals also help prevent brain disorders like depression and Alzheimer's disease (Ahmad et al., 2021).

Here's a list of healthy foods you can include in your child's diet to enhance your child's brain function:

- **Carbohydrates:** Bread, rice, whole grains, starchy vegetables, beans, legumes, berries, beetroot, etc.
- **Others:** salmon, mackerel, nuts, flaxseed, sardines, dark chocolate, coffee, turmeric, eggs, etc.

You can also include fatty food and dairy products but a moderate amount. Some unhealthy meals for your child's brain include junk food, barbecue or other smoked foods, cookies, ice cream, fried foods, soda and other sugary drinks, processed foods, etc. Excessive intake of these can affect your brain negatively.

Sleep and ADHD

People with ADHD have it hard in many areas of their lives, and that includes their sleep pattern. They are either unable to fall asleep, have nightmares when they do sleep, or have problems waking up. Their sleep pattern is uncertain and can lead to a sleep disorder.

Some scientists posit that it may be the result of an irregular or delayed circadian rhythm. This sleep disorder starts in ADHD patients as early as 12 years old. For the predominantly hyperactive ones, they can't fall asleep. They mostly suffer from insomnia, which leads to other problems during the day. That's because their minds and bodies are always active and restless.

For those with predominant inattention, they fall asleep way after bedtime. They may lie down, but it'll take hours before they can sleep. In the combined cases, they can't have little or no sleep, with nightmares and difficulty in waking up.

Lack of sleep, even for a neurotypical, can cause migraines, a lack of concentration, and forgetfulness. These are already things ADHD patients suffer from. Adding a lack of proper sleep to it only worsens the case. It keeps them confused, lost, irritated, unfocused, anxious, and forgetful throughout the day.

The more it persists, especially for the chronic cases, the more depressed they get. They'll begin to have bursts of daytime sleepiness. They can be in class and just fall asleep. They can no longer control how, when, or where they fall asleep. That's because the body needs a certain amount of rest to function.

This can be a very dangerous state because, an adult, may be in a meeting at the office or driving, and they can just fall asleep. It can result in the loss of a job or a fatal accident.

However, there are stimulants that help ADHD patients sleep better. This stimulant releases a calm feeling in them, and when they're calm, they can easily fall asleep. However, some people may find stimulants more sleep-repellent than sleep-inducing.

If you're having trouble putting your ADHD child to sleep, there are other ways, aside from taking drugs you can adopt. Firstly, establish a nighttime routine - time for food, type of food, quantity of food, and time for sleep. You don't want to fill up their stomachs before bed, as that can make them feel uncomfortable.

When it's getting close to their bedtime, their mind knows because of the routine. You can take them to bed, lie them down, turn off all lights, and read them a story. A hug and a goodnight kiss will also help. For some others, having a glass of milk helps.

You should use different methods and see which works for your child. It's really important that you help your child work on their sleeping issue so it doesn't affect their life.

Takeaway Two

ADHD kids are always seen in a negative light, and they get negative comments almost every day. The more they hear this, the more they believe it, and this belief, if not corrected on time, will go on to shape their lives.

The clay that reshapes these negative beliefs into positive ones is their superpower. ADHD kids have great potential, and what seems to be their defect - hyperactivity, impulsiveness, and inattention - can become a force for their good.

They just need to be guided so they can channel their hyperactivity into doing something profitable. When they begin to see their strengths more than their weaknesses, they'll live better lives.

Chapter 3

Mindful Parenting Techniques

Listen earnestly to anything [your children] want to tell you, no matter what. If you don't listen eagerly to the little stuff when they are little, they won't tell you the big stuff when they are big, because to them all of it has always been big stuff.
— **Catherine M. Wallace**

How effective can mindfulness be in parenting an ADHD child? A study conducted and published in 2017 in the Journal of Developmental and Behavioral Pediatrics ascertains its effectiveness. And I can establish this too with the experience of an ADHD parent.

Emily (not her real name) had the responsibility of raising an ADHD Max all by herself. Being a single mom was a lot. But having to deal with a child with special needs compounded parenthood for her. Having to give her full attention at work and respond to calls from her son's school was tearing her apart. She had to deal with a high level of stress every day. She was coping well until she broke down mentally.

Emily had no choice other than to seek professional help. That was when she knew what her child was dealing with. And one of the techniques she was introduced to was mindfulness. This technique wasn't just for her son, but for her as well. Gradually, mother and son began to understand their mental and emotional shifts and how to deal with them.

This could be it for you too. The good thing is that you don't need an external facility to practice this technique. Pay attention to its application in the following sections.

Mindfulness and Its Role in Parenting ADHD

Parenting ADHD kids has its good times, but also its tough times. As a parent, you need to employ a way of unwinding, because accumulation of stress can be hazardous to your health. One very effective way to unwind is by practicing mindfulness.

Mindfulness is a state of being and thinking only about the present happenings around you without feeling guilty about it. There are mindfulness meditation techniques that bring you to the present and make you feel and focus your mind on what is happening at the present. Mindfulness cleanses your mind of past irritation, anxiety, and unease. It brings your mind to focus on your present need and that of your ADHD kid.

It also improves your circadian rhythm, regulates high blood pressure, and increases your productivity. You see, the mind is one of your key points. It's where your emotions will reside. If anything negative enters and stays there, it'll affect not just your mind but your health, lifestyle, actions, and mood.

Anything that doesn't affect your mind, won't have the power to alter your mood. So you need to raise a healthy mind by watching what you listen to, and what you see. But greater than what you see or hear is how you interpret situations, and that's based on the beliefs you hold dear. Mindfulness helps you reposition your mind to receive only profitable things.

This type of meditation makes you feel calm, more understanding, a good listener, and all these enable you to make better judgments about the present situation. This way, you don't act or react in the present based on accumulated stress. (Wong, 2022)

Your mind only interprets and judges the situation at the present based on what you can see now. For instance, if you've tried teaching your ADHD adolescent to pick up after himself but he refuses to learn, it may add to your stress.

If you see him leaving his shoes or clothes on the floor once he enters the house, you will react harshly based on the stress of all the times you've had to pick after him and instructed him to do it himself.

However, as you develop the habit of mindful meditation, you will no longer feel that burden of past corrections. So when you see him leave his shoes behind in the present, it'll feel like this is the first time you're correcting him.

So when you correct him in the present, you'll do it mildly and with love. You'll also be patient with him as you watch him pick his shoes. Invariably, mindfulness helps the parent maintain sanity and peace of mind.

Adopting parenting mindfulness lets you keep your focus on your family. It helps you prioritize your emotions. If making your ADHD child feel loved is your goal, you'll know to control your temper when they do something wrong.

You would check the tone of voice you use in correcting or helping them. You'll be watchful of your actions around them too. This helps you make a better judgment because instead of shouting at their wrongdoing, you'd be patient enough to hear them out and know the reason for their misbehavior.

This way, you'll be able to tell them better ways of doing that whenever they're faced with such problems in the future. You're training them.

However, there are certain things you need to know about mindfulness meditation. It's not magic. It's a process that can take from months to years before you can get the best experience from it. The key is consistency.

There's a rule of mindfulness that states that you must practice it twice a day. First thing in the morning before breakfast for 20-30 minutes, and also at night before you sleep. It's to be observed twice daily, compulsorily, for it to be effective in the long run.

To practice mindfulness, you need a mantra and a quiet place. Firstly, sit in a quiet place. If you don't have any quiet area around, anywhere will do. Noise won't disrupt your mindfulness. When you're seated comfortably, close your eyes and allow your mind to relax. If thoughts and images start coming to your mind, let them.

After a minute or two, begin to listen to and recite your mantra. If you have a headphone, use it. It'll be better than listening to it without one. Continue to recite it and let it overshadow any thoughts coming up. When you're done, lay down quietly for 5 minutes.

This kind of meditation has a purpose and that is to release your mind. While you meditate, if you sleep off, it's fine. When you wake, do it and then rest for 5 minutes. You need to do it twice daily, consistently for a year or two.

Know that you can't force the result. It just happens. It creeps in slowly and one day, you'll just notice you're a lot calmer and more patient with your ADHD child. You'll also be able to communicate effectively with others. You'll be a lot happier and healthier.

Nevertheless, there's a caution about this kind of meditation. You may encounter tempting situations immediately after meditating. It's like these situations come to test if the meditation is working. For instance, after meditation, that's when you'll see your child with ADHD run to the kitchen, carry a plate of food carelessly and it pours.

Or you'll just see something that pisses you off. At that point, you have to remind yourself of your new journey of peace and overlook it. Don't respond to that situation then. Just walk away, and when you're feeling a lot calmer, you can address the issue.

There's one thing you should understand. Humans differ and so does their body configuration. If you don't find mindfulness meditation helpful, or if it even worsens the case by getting you all worked up because you're not sure you're doing it right, then stop doing it.

You can try other stress-relieving activities like yoga, reading, hanging out with friends, karaoke, walking, or even eating what you crave at that time. Engage in whatever makes you happy.

Practicing Patience and Active Listening

Patience and active listening are both soft skills that will save you from getting into a lot of trouble. Patience is the ability to wait it out with the right attitude. But it's not just about waiting, but also about your attitude as you wait. It's your attitude and ability to wait that shows whether or not you have patience.

That's because patience is a thing of the mind. It's indeed about how you react outwardly, but more than outwardly is how you react inwardly. Once your inside is screaming, it's only a matter of time and the right push, you'll soon start screaming outwardly.

So in waiting patiently, your body and mind must be in sync. It's not easy to practice patience. It takes a conscious effort to do it, and the contradiction here is that it doesn't come naturally to man. Patience is not a gift, it's a skill that is learned which can later become part of you after much conscious practice.

See, humans are programmed to respond and react on impulse. But when you're patient, you don't react immediately. You'll have the ability to hold on to your reaction till you've heard what the other person has to say. Then you'd be able to give a better judgment. Impulsive reactions can cause a lot of trouble.

For instance, let's say you get a call from your ADHD teen's school. You rush down there and you learn that he fought with another student. Maybe this is the first time it's happening, maybe not. That's not the point. Now, you go home with him and before the door is shut behind you, you begin to scold him.

You don't care to know the reason why he did what he did. You're just caught up in the stress of everything you've been facing, the sacrifices you've made for him, and now, you feel betrayed that he'd do that, knowing he'd get a suspension. You react based on all of these going on in your mind.

At this point, even if you start crying as a mom, you're losing the battle. If your son is sympathetic enough, he may apologize, but you've lost him. That's because you hadn't developed the virtue of patience.

Parenting ADHD with Empathy And Effectiveness

Now, there's a reason for everything, and the reason is what really matters, not what happened. Therein lies the difference between patience and impatience. While impatience judges what happened (the problem at hand), patience judges the "Why" of the problem (the root).

Using the example above, if you have developed patience, your reaction will be different. Now, while it's true you're hurt about the fight and suspension, you'll think beyond that and your focus will be on your son.

Patience will lead you to think, Why would he do this? What could have prompted him to make such a decision without minding the consequences? You know he's not a monster that bullies for fun. And even if he is, something actually made him that way. If you can tackle what made him that way, you will never catch him fighting again.

That's a more constructive way to think. So, just like every offender, your son will be expecting a scolding that he'd just accept and go up to his room and brood. But patience uses another tactic. When you get home, you can just give him a hug. Let him shower, and prepare a good meal for him.

During that period, he's waiting for the bait he thinks you're trying to pass out. He's ready to sink. But when he goes to bed and you still haven't spoken about it, he'd feel guilty and come talk to you. If he doesn't, you can go to his room, sit gently beside him, and ask him what really happened.

You may be surprised to find out that the other guy at school has probably been bullying him because of his condition for so long, and that day, he may have said something too painful to bear. When you learn the problem, see it from his eyes. Understand why he got so angry, and then support him.

Now, your aim is to pass a message. You can't do that if you're an opponent. So, you can say something like this:

They don't deserve you at that school. You're too good for them. Sorry darling (or whatever pet name you wish to call him) you had to go through that.

When you've said this, he will feel more relaxed and open to whatever you wish to say again. Then you can say:

Mindful Parenting Techniques

I know it hurts, but you know you're better than them in so many ways. For starters, they can't play chess like you do (mention something he loves and is really good at). So next time, when they say hurtful things, look them in the eye, laugh, and walk away. When your opponent sees he's not getting to you, he'd feel ashamed of himself. So, you win without even having to beat him up.

This will bring a smile to his face and peace to his heart. With the tactics of patience, you've been able to know a part of your son you never knew, given him a way out of a difficulty he's been worried about, and proven to him you love him. This alone will bring you both closer.

When you react like this a couple of times, you'll notice he'd begin to open up to you without you even asking. He may say it sometimes like he's angry at someone or something, or he may just mention it to you. In those instances, support him, then advise him. As a child with ADHD, they're very sensitive and they want to know you're on their side.

On the other hand, you need to practice the skill of active listening. Active listening is listening to someone with your mind and body to understand what the person is about. When you listen actively, your focus is on the person's perspective. You're not listening and then your mind is thinking of how to respond to each point.

This is supposed to be the easiest kind of listening, but it's the most difficult kind. It takes discipline and patience to do this, because humans love talking about themselves, not about others. But if they have to listen to someone talk, they're prone to giving advice or suggestions.

With this nature, it's hard to be an active listener, because you'd have something in mind you want to contribute or advice. But active listening should be easy because it demands little or nothing from you. All it demands is your genuine interest, a few gestures here and there to show you're listening, and a smile or nod at some point (Narins, 2023).

It demands nothing else. So you don't have to stress your mind thinking up a solution or advice. That's easy, right?

Parenting ADHD with Empathy And Effectiveness

Active listening helps you make the right decision and judgment. It opens your eyes to see from a different perspective.

As a parent of an ADHD child, you need this skill. Your child will talk a lot, and shushing them every time will push them away from you. It's not their fault. It's the nature of their condition. So you need to learn to listen with an open mind and with interest.

You can get genuinely interested by asking the "WH" questions - Why, What, When, Where. When they start talking about a girl in school or a teacher in their class, ask them questions that'll get them to keep talking constructively. Questions like,

- Why did he do that?
- Wow, when will they come?
- How did it happen?
- What did you do?

These questions not only help you gain interest in the topic, it also guides them in their speech. So, instead of talking about a teacher in school, and then jumping to talking about what they saw in the garden, they're able to talk about the teacher and all that happened, before moving on to a different subject. So the discussion is not scattered.

Patience is needed in active listening, and if you can do that for your ADHD child, you'll score a big point with your child. They'll find it easy to confide in you whenever they're faced with real challenges, or when they're going through a phase.

You see, parents think that providing all a child needs is what makes you close to them, but ut that's not it. Your child needs to feel your impact in their lives, personally, beyond money and food. What they remember about you, or what makes them miss you when you go on a trip, are those times you listened to them, cuddled them and advised them.

It's those personal moments that makes you their friend. That's what draws a child close. That's why you need to learn and practice patience and active listening. It'll help you connect more with your kid(s).

Stress Reduction Strategies for Parents

Parenting is a beautiful experience. It's one thing most parents crave for. But we all know kids can be a handful. ADHD kids, on the other hand, are more than a handful. That's because their nature opposes the daily routine of a neurotypical.

Parenting an ADHD child means cleaning up after them, always watching them so they don't harm themselves, having trouble putting them to sleep, and having to deal with the fact that they may do poorly academically, and at home, they can't obey your instructions because they can't even remember them.

This is hard for parents because you know they can't help it, so you just have to find ways to deal with it. At first, you may try to ignore the irritationyou feel within, but when other kids start coming and the workload increases, especially for mothers, you just find yourself snapping at every turn.

Whether you're a stay-at-home parent, or a career one, the stress follows you everywhere. When you have to deal with your ADHD kid and your other kids, work, house chores, cooking, shopping, and then still make time for your spouse, it can be a lot. The stress will accumulate over time, and if you don't do anything to relieve it, depression and anxiety may set in.

Therefore, as a parent, you have to devise ways of relieving yourself and your ADHD child of stress, because if they feel relieved, it'll also benefit you. Here are some stress reduction strategies you can adopt:

- **Take it a day at a time:** Stress comes from worrying about tomorrow or what might happen later. But one thing about worrying is that it doesn't make the present better or solve the problem. Stop worrying about what might or might not happen to your child. Stop worrying about what you're doing or not doing right. Just focus on the moment and deal with the current challenges one after another.

- **Set a routine:** Setting a routine for the family will help your ADHD child and keep your family in check. Everyone knows when it's bedtime, mealtime, reading time, etc.

- **Delegate duties:** If you have other neurotypical kids aside from the one with ADHD, assign duties to them. You can even make a duty roster - who washes the dishes, takes out the trash, vacuums the floor, and takes care of the ADHD child each day. So everyone knows whose turn it is to take care of the ADHD kid and pick up after him, help clean his room, play with him, and keep him in check at home. You can even put your kids in the same school so they can watch out for their ADHD brother at school.

- **Set family fun time:** This is important especially if you have other kids aside from your ADHD kid. Family fun time brings everyone together. It helps cover the lapses you may have with other kids so they don't feel like you only care about and give all your love to their ADHD sibling. It can be family game night or movie night.

- **Individual time:** Individual time is the time you spend with each child. Remember, if you spend all the time talking about or assigning your ADHD child to your other children, they'll feel left out. This can make them act harshly and increase their stress. So, to help with that, you can pick an activity that you will do with each child. It can be that you always cook with your first child, and garden with your last. You can go shopping with the second. It all depends on how many you have, but have that fun intimate moment where it's just the two of you.

- **Self-love/care:** You can't keep giving without receiving, and when I say receiving, I'm not necessarily talking about the support you get from your spouse or friends and relatives. I'm talking about self-support. You need to create time for yourself. A time you can relax and do what you like. It can be when the kids go to school, or when everyone is off to bed. You can just sit and read a book or do something you like. Take yourself out and have fun. It has a way of rejuvenating you every time.

- **Seek support:** Don't be ashamed to ask for help from your neighbors, family, friends, and even your kid's teachers at school. You can't bear the burden of raising and watching an ADHD child alone. Accept their help to watch them while you go do other things. Send your kids to grandma's or your relatives for holidays or some weekends.

- **Impact knowledge:** From time to time, enlighten your kids and family about the peculiarities of ADHD. Ensure they understand why they have to help. When they do, they'll help out without complaint. Also, teach your ADHD child how to socialize. You can start by helping him make friends with the kids in your neighborhood, then at school. It'll make them live happier, and that's a win for you.

- **Healthy lifestyle:** It's important you inculcate a healthy lifestyle into your family. Set a routine for family exercise, set a diet plan (that of your ADHD kid will be different to fit their need), and encourage healthy communication in the family. Teach your kids how to communicate with love, patience, respect, and understanding.

Stress can make you look older than your age, always agitated, increase blood pressure, anxious, and can lead to depression. That's why you have to tackle it using these strategies.

There are lots of benefits to handling stress:

- Improved appetite
- Always happy and at peace with yourself
- Tolerance and patience
- A happy family
- A more peaceful sleep
- Healthy living and lifestyle

- Improved productivity

Mindful Communication with Your Child

When it comes to communication, kids tend to relate more with their peers rather than their parents. That's because they feel their parents don't understand how they feel. They see parents as ancient people trying to fit in a modern world.

A teen girl will find it easier talking to a friend about the guy she has a crush on than talking to her mom. A teen boy will either talk to his friends, read about it, or keep his conflicting emotions to himself about the changes in his body that he can't understand. When you ask why they won't talk to their parents, the answer is mostly, "They WON'T understand".

Well, the truth is, they are almost always right. See, as a parent, you have gone through some things growing up. You know how you associated with a bad group and they almost got you in trouble. You remember sneaking out of the house as a teen girl to go party with some friends just because they insisted you come. You remember some stupid things you did as a teen simply because your friends dared you to.

As an adult, you will naturally want to protect your kids from those experiences. So, you may catch yourself shouting more than talking to them, always judging their every move, setting strict rules, and some parents go as far as banning their kids from doing anything outside schoolwork. All these restrictions and checks are what sets a chasm between you and your kids.

You need to understand that every phase of life has its peculiarities and drives. You may be an adult and know better, but your kids are still young and don't know any better. That's life. This is why you need to learn mindful communication with your kids, especially if you have one with ADHD.

Mindful communication is the act of having an open and honest conversation with your child, and seeing from their perspective without being judgemental. This type of communication helps you truly see and know your child beyond their name or what they had for breakfast.

In this communication, your tone, gesture, facial expression, and reaction matter a lot. According to facts, nonverbal communication is 93% above verbal. (as cited in, Goally, 2023). So, your kids don't just hear what you say, they see your reaction.

If they tell you something, or you find out something about them, the way you react will determine what they will tell you in the future. They may likely restrict communication to only what you need to know or permit.

Mindful communication opens up your child to you, and you can now see their fears, desires, and ambitions. You begin to not just understand what is happening in their lives, but how they feel about everything.

You get it wrong when you think you know your child just because you know how they are doing at school, the food they eat, the friends they keep, and when they are sad or happy. Knowing someone goes beyond what is currently happening. It's knowing how they feel. Your child may be doing well in science but it may not be what they want to do.

They may only be doing that because you want it from them and they want to make you proud. Take for instance the story of a lady who graduated with a first class in Medicine. After graduation, she took her certificate and gave it to her father. She told him that she studied Medicine for him because that's what he wanted. Then she went off to study what she wanted to study.

So, when it comes to kids, you can't just conclude based on what you see. Find time to sit with your child (ADHD or not), take a deep breath with them, and then share your feelings. You can do this in their room at night. It can be in a private area.

If you notice your daughter or son acting strangely, don't just wave it off. Something has happened. You can take them out to the park, or a restaurant and start an open and honest conversation. Ask them how they feel about school, their other siblings, your and your spouse's parenting approach, etc.

Parenting ADHD with Empathy And Effectiveness

Just ask questions that will make them open up about how they really feel. You can do this from time to time, maybe every year on their birthday.

As you listen to them, remember, that the aim is not to judge or advise them on the spot to "set them right". As you listen, nod, ask questions that'll make them talk more, paraphrase their words and say them back to them so they know you're both on the same page, and most importantly, never belittle their feelings. Instead, validate their feelings.

You can share your experiences in the past and how you felt to validate their feelings. When they say something that seems childish, don't laugh at how they feel. That'll turn them off. Make them know that their feelings are valid.

However, this is not a practice for the weak in the heart. If you want them to open up about how they truly feel, you should be ready to hear things you never imagined and still maintain your cool. You may discover that your child has gay tendencies, is no longer a virgin, or drinks with friends, etc. You need to be strong so you don't end up spoiling the mindful communication with your outburst.

Besides, your reaction is what will determine if mindful communication is effective or not.

In practicing mindful communication, your motive and goal matter a lot. You need to have a reason for doing it. What do you hope to get out of it? How can you use it to help?

Your goal and motive can be to get closer to your kids and guide them better in making the right choices. Remember as a parent, your function in your child's life is not to dictate how they are to live, it's to guide them into the right path. You need to keep in mind that although they're your kids, they're also humans. They have self-will, likes and dislikes, so you can't control them.

As they grow, you need to understand them and why they act the way they do. To help, you can do research about the changes children undergo at different periods. It'll help you understand the hormones responsible for what they feel. You'll also know what to expect and guide them with that knowledge.

For instance, as your teen daughter approaches 10-12 years old, you can start giving them small talks about menstruation and prepare their minds. Tell them what it looks like, how it comes, and the reason for it. Tell her the implication when it starts. This way, when it happens, you'll be the first person on her mind to reach out to.

As she approaches 16-18 years, you can begin to enlighten her about the changes that her body will begin to undergo. Your spouse can do the same with the male children. This way, you will form a stronger bond with your kids.

Reducing Blame and Guilt: Parental Self-Care and Wellbeing

Blame and guilt are two feelings that almost all parents are familiar with. These feelings make you as a parent (of a neurotypical kid or neurodiverse kid) feel incompetent, lacking, and responsible for anything your kid does or goes through.

Kids are prone to making mistakes, and as they become teenagers, that possibility increases. ADHD kids on the other hand have a nature that makes them hyperactive, impulsive, and inattentive, so they're prone to more harmful stunts.

If you have an ADHD child, you may feel guilty as to why they were born like that. You will feel it's your fault, and whenever they do some embarrassing things in public, you'll take the blame for it. If it's not checked, you may blame yourself all through your life because your pain is valid.

As a parent, you feel you know better and you actually try all you can to help your kids make the right choices, however, it may not always happen. You may begin to feel guilty or blame yourself because you feel you're not meeting up as a parent. You may feel you're too strict with your rules, or that you're not balancing your work and family life properly.

You take responsibility for everyone's actions around you and you are constantly beating yourself up, trying to meet up with your kids, making them feel loved, your spouse, your work, and making everyone around you happy.

These feelings can make you feel constantly unhappy, and irritated, and can cause headache and depression. One other thing about the feeling of guilt and blame is that they don't solve any problem. They only add to your stress and make you feel constantly frustrated. No matter how much you try to set things right so you can be accepted, nothing ever seems to be enough.

It's like you're beating the wind. You keep trying and getting more frustrated. It seems like there's always another ladder to climb. You wish sometimes that you had a different family, maybe it would have been better. This negative attitude will create a gulf between you and your family.

Problems will begin to arise because in trying to be free, you'd begin to pass the blame around. You'd begin to see ways others aren't meeting up to help you out, and it's just shouting all day long.

The feeling of guilt does a lot more damage to you than the family you're feeling guilty about. However, there's a positive guilt. This is a constructive criticism and analysis of your family and the decisions you've taken. You can even engage the whole family.

Everyone will be free to air their opinions on what they like and what they dislike. You can then see what needs to be changed and find better ways of doing them. Or better still, you can share your concerns with your spouse and join heads to tackle the issues.

To overcome guilt, you need to take a moment to analyze what is your fault and what isn't. For instance, if you have ADHD and one of your kids has it too, you can't blame yourself because you didn't choose to have it, nor did you choose to pass it on. That's not something you can control.

Mindful Parenting Techniques

Instead of focusing on what you can't change, think of how to handle the present challenge. Seek solutions and better ways to make your child feel better. Some medications and therapies can help an ADHD child live and act almost normally.

When you find solutions, apply them. Don't give excuses about what may or may not have worked in the past or for someone else. You don't want to bother about what might be. You want to focus on what can be.

Instead of seeing the weaknesses of your ADHD child, see his strengths. For instance, instead of thinking, *He has some potential but his restlessness increases every day, and he is doing too poorly at school*; think, *He may not be doing too well at school and is getting restless, but his ability to focus is getting better, he's happier, and he's very good at chess now. He'd win me one day if he continued like this.*

The first line of thought minimizes his strengths and spotlights his weaknesses. While the second spotlights his strengths and minimizes his weaknesses. This may look like it doesn't matter, but I tell you, if you can think like the latter, you'll suddenly begin to see all the beauty in your child and his mistakes will seem like something that doesn't really matter.

In addition, you should take care of yourself and don't feel guilty about it. Eat healthy meals, take a lot of water, take evening walks, go to the park, and go see a movie. Do Whatever you need to do, that'll make you happy. Being happy doesn't mean you don't care about your kids. It shows that you respect and love yourself, therefore, you'd know how to respect and care for your kids.

Whether or not you live in blame and guilt all your life as a parent depends on your mindset. Think positive thoughts, see the best in what you do and see how important you are to your kids. Don't judge or look down on your effort. Don't let society judge how you raise your kids. Just ensure everyone, including yourself, is happy, disciplined, and respectful, and you'll have done your bit.

If your kids make mistakes, don't make them feel like they are a mistake, or blame yourself. Simply address the issue independently and give the necessary discipline. You can later tell them why what they did is wrong and why you had to punish them. This way, everyone is happy.

Takeaway Three

Parenting can be a handful and overwhelming, whether you're parenting neurotypicals or neurodiverse kids. As a parent, you will face the challenge of communicating productively with your kids, sharing the love equally, meeting up at work, and still caring for your spouse and friends.

For better efficiency in parenting, you need to find ways to unwind from time to time. You can practice mindfulness, meditation, and empathic communication. It'll help you live in the present, be more understanding, patient, calm, and make wiser judgements. It'll also strengthen your parent-child relationship.

Part 2

Empowering Your Child's Development

Your kids are one of your most valuable "assets", that's why you need to take the time to invest heavily and intentionally in them. For your ADHD kids, you want to be particular in helping them with control of their emotions so they don't push everyone away.

Therefore, learning practical ways to help your child manage their emotions, become more focused, and more organized, and exercise self-control are some of the best gifts you can give them.

You're about to experience something phenomenal in your parenting journey.

Chapter 4

Embracing Emotional Regulation

"In between every action and reaction, there is a space. Usually, the space is extremely small because we react so quickly, but take notice of that space and expand it. Be aware in that space that you have a choice to make. You can choose how to respond, and choose wisely, because the next step you take will teach your child how to handle anger and could either strengthen or damage your relationship."
— **Rebecca Eanes**

Emotional Dysregulation in ADHD

Emotion is common to humans, but that of ADHD kids is more intense than that of neurotypicals. An estimated 25-45% of kids and 30-70% of adults suffer from emotional dysregulation (Astenvald et al., 2022). This is mainly due to the configuration of their brain.

In a neurotypical brain, the amygdala receives emotions in its raw and heightened form and sends them to other parts of the brain, especially the prefrontal cortex. The cerebral cortex examines the intensity of the emotion and regulates it. If the issue isn't serious, it diffuses the emotions. That's why you are able to control your temper or otherwise. In a case where you have a task to perform, after performing the task, dopamine (responsible for rewarding the brain), is released so you feel good about yourself.

This is not the same in the neurodiverse brain. The link between the amygdala and the prefrontal cortex is weak in a neurodiverse brain. So the emotions come out as intense and raw as they are in the amygdala. Therefore, an ADHD child cannot tell when a situation is serious or not. They react to all the feelings that come.

Embracing Emotional Regulation

For instance, if you say, "No," to the craving of a normal child, they may whine a bit and stop, irrespective of how much they want that thing. But if you do that to an ADHD child, they may cry so hard or be really sad and angry that you'd think you did something more than saying, "No."

But the good thing about the emotions of an ADHD child is that they're easily appeased and it doesn't take long for the emotional display to wear out. However, when they get angry, they throw serious tantrums. They may hit something or even hurt themselves.

This kind of uncontrolled emotional outburst is called emotional dysregulation. It means an inability to regulate or control emotions. ADHD kids are very sensitive to criticism, disapproval, and rejection. In fact, they don't even need to be criticized to feel bad. Even if they perceive it from friends, family, or peers, they react immediately. They are what you call, touchy.

Due to their high sensitivity to the words and the reactions of others, they easily develop rejection-sensitive dysphoria (RSD). It means it's hard for them to bear rejection. It's almost like a phobia. Due to this, they try to please everyone. At home, they try their best to do things correctly, like their neurotypical siblings, so they don't get scolded.

At school, they're self-conscious of their hyperactivity and try their best to move as little as possible. They may begin to hate themselves because they can't even control what people taunt them about. They develop low self-esteem and soon lose themselves in the process.

But that's not the case for all of them. While some hide in their shells their whole lives, others take to defiance. They begin to respond to every insult, scolding, and rejection with anger and hate. They point out the faults in others so they can hate them and feel better.

As they grow, they can't remember who they are or what they like because they've spent all their lives doing what other people approve of or trying to piss others off. They also get depressed because, despite the effort they've put into trying to be accepted, it never works.

They find out that they are only trying to survive. They can't take on difficult tasks, so they remain a stereotype. They also can't maintain friendships because of these emotional outbursts that don't care about how others feel until it's expressed.

The Emotion-ADHD Connection: Nurturing Emotional Intelligence

ADHD kids are known for their intense and sometimes aggressive emotional responses. They have no self-control, or emotional control. When they express anger, they may say or do hurtful things without thinking about how the other person feels. They're unable to stop until they've done what is on their mind to do.

This affects their relationships, academics, lifestyle, mindset, and self-esteem. They can't maintain friendships, and because of this, they choose isolation and self-pity. If not helped, these kids will either attempt suicide to end the pain and struggle, become a nuisance to drown the pain, or simply live in isolation.

But they don't have to be like this all their lives. There are ways you, as a parent, can help them develop emotional intelligence. Emotional intelligence (EI) is the ability to control one's emotions, apply them correctly and to the right degree, understand the emotions of others, and empathize with them.

As a parent, you can start by teaching your ADHD child the different types of emotions and their triggers. You can use pictures, movies, or facial expressions to visualize your lesson. Show them an angry face and what causes one to be angry. Show them a sad face, a scared face, a happy face, etc. You can also ask them to make such faces.

After teaching them the triggers in the most understanding way, practice it with them. You can say something and ask them to react with the right reaction and intensity. When they do, you can then enlighten them on why people will say that to them and how they should take it so they don't react angrily.

Embracing Emotional Regulation

Secondly, teach them to accept themselves. Every day, show them the beauty in their disorder. Tell them why they act the way they do and teach them to accept it because it's only when they accept it that they can attempt to control it. That's also when they will see themselves in a new light, and what people say won't affect them so much. This way, you're building self-confidence in them.

Again, prepare their minds for the likely challenges they'll face at home and outside the house. Enlighten them that not everyone will accept them, but they shouldn't fail to see those who do. Let them know that they may be bullied at school, misinterpreted, or face rejection from their peers, but it shouldn't make them feel less of a person. Teach them that they are defined by what they think about themselves and not what others say.

Let them know that everyone has one flaw or another, some more pronounced than others. It doesn't mean they should hate themselves or condemn others. Let them know that they can be great people in life. Read stories of people with ADHD who became great in life. You can make them listen to a motivational podcast that's specific to them.

The more they hear positive words about themselves from their family and from podcasts, the more confident they'll be. They'll accept themselves and interpret life differently. You can also write and paste short quotes all over their room. They should say one each day before they leave the house. At school or anywhere else, if they hear a negative comment, they should recite that quote for the day. It'll help calm their temper.

Also, teach them that others also have emotions. Due to their peculiarity, they feel others are fine, and they are the ones with the problem. They don't think normal people have troubles or face challenges. So when they are rejected by normal kids, their emotions are heightened, and they say all the hurtful things they can think of so it will hurt the other person.

So, you need to teach them that others also have feelings. Teach them that normal people feel pain, anger, hate, joy, and fear too, just like them. Teach them ways of responding to the actions of others. Teach them maturity in silence and walking away from bullies. Let them know that if they are criticized at school or anywhere else, not saying anything and walking away makes them win because it makes the other person look stupid.

Another way you can help them build emotional intelligence is by teaching them to journal their thoughts and feelings. They can carry their journal everywhere they go. Instead of responding to someone's criticism, they should go somewhere quiet and write it down. After a while, they should read and analyze the reactions they wrote down and see if they are targeted to hurt the other person.

Let them know that practicing emotional intelligence is not in any way to make them look good before others, be accepted, or fit in. No. If that was it, it'd mean that they're living for others. And that's not what this book advocates. They need to practice EI for their own well-being and peace of mind. It's so they can be proud of themselves. They need to understand that spitting on others won't make them feel better or become normal. It'll only turn them into monsters, and they don't want that.

You need to give them reasons for the actions you advise them to take so they know why they have to do them when they're faced with a challenge. You can also teach them to practice mindfulness meditation. When they seem tense or perceive criticism, instead of reacting, they should take deep breaths until they feel calm.

In addition, you can encourage them to participate in social events. Let them practice what to say and how to interact with people at home before they go out. Also, teach them how to apologize to those they may have hurt with their words. Teach them ways to maintain friends, even if it's one or two.

In helping them with tasks, break them down. If a project seems bulky, it discourages them, but when you break it down into small bits, the task will seem easier to carry out.

As a parent, I know that this sounds easy, but it'll take a long time to get used to these new routines. It may take months or years before your ADHD child can show signs of EI because they're literally fighting against their nature. So, be patient with them, and teach them to be patient with themselves and the process. They shouldn't get frustrated when they can't help but express their emotions.

Mindful Breathing Techniques: Calming the Storm Within

Stress is a part of our everyday lives. It starts from when we wake up to when we sleep. When we wake, we're thinking of what the day will bring, how to go about our tasks for the day, how to react appropriately, and how to manage the family for the day. Every activity seems to place a demand on our emotions.

Stress can be acute or chronic. Acute stress is a temporary emotional disturbance while chronic stress lasts longer. When we hear stress most times, we think of a negative feeling. It's not always like that. There is a positive stress called eustress. This kind of stress motivates us to carry out tasks and boosts our morale. However, there is also negative stress that makes us anxious, depressed, frustrated, and uneasy.

We all experience this kind of stress almost every day, both adults and kids. It's even worse for kids because they haven't developed the ability to manage their emotions. But for ADHD kids and their parents (including their siblings), negative stress doubles. This is because they all have to watch over their ADHD child/sibling and put up with their fracas. That's stressful.

Nevertheless, irrespective of the type of stress you're going through, you need a way to calm the storm raging within so you don't transfer the aggression to others and mess up your relationships. One of the best and most effective ways of releasing stress is through mindfulness breathing techniques. It works for both adults and kids alike.

Practicing any of these techniques will lighten your mind, help you focus on the present, relieve you of stress, anger, fear, and anxiety, and lead you gradually out of depression (if you've gotten to that stage). Practicing these techniques doesn't change the things that happen to you every day, but it changes the way you perceive and reacts to them.

So you'll notice that what normally gets you worked up no longer does. You'll begin to notice you talk more calmly while correcting your kids, and you smile and hum more. It seems like nothing seems to bother you anymore. It makes you happier, healthier, and calmer.

Here are four mindful breathing techniques you and your kids should try:

- **Mindful breathing:** This is different from normal breathing only because of its intentionality. You can sit in a comfortable position, stand, or lie straight on your back. Then, you want to take in air through your nose for three seconds, hold it for two seconds, and then release it through your mouth in four seconds. The aim is to be conscious of your breathing in the present. Focus on your inhaling and exhaling, the time it takes, your position, where your hand is, and yourself. You don't have to force the breathing or regulate it. Just let it flow freely. Do this for at least 5-7 minutes every day.

- **7/11 technique:** You can easily practice this with your kid.. Your ADHD kid will benefit more because it's best for people who are under a lot of pressure like police officers, the navy, CEOs, teachers, etc. Now, sit with your kids and let everyone be calm. Then inhale slowly for 7 seconds, and exhale slowly for 11 seconds. Do this for as many times as you can simultaneously. You'll feel an immediate release and calming of the rage within you.

- **Deep breathing:** You should do this when you're feeling sad, frustrated, really pissed, or under pressure. However, doing it daily will also help. You can sit, stand, lie on your back, or whatever position you're most comfortable in. Now, take a deep breath from your diaphragm. It shouldn't come from your chest, but from deep inside your belly. As you inhale slowly, your belly will rise. Hold the breath for 3-5 seconds, then release slowly. It gives your brain the signal to calm down and that nothing has gone wrong.

- **The "SEAT" breathing technique:** This is more than just breathing. It's also a self-examining exercise that helps you check your feelings,

Embracing Emotional Regulation

dissect them, and calm down. SEAT is an acronym for Sensation, Emotions, Actions, and Thoughts. You sit comfortably, close your eyes, take a deep breath, and then focus your mind on the sensations you feel, the emotions bursting inside you presently, the actions you plan to take to address these emotions, and the thoughts you have about yourself or about the cause of these bursting emotions. When you focus on these, you'll see how vain these emotions are, and you'll be able to examine your actions and see how negative or positive your thoughts are. The result of your examination will tell if you should go on and react to the emotion, or let it go.

These techniques work better when you do it daily and for the right amount of time. When you practice it daily for weeks or months, it'll become a part of you. You can practice any of these techniques anytime you're in a fix, or you're about to lose your temper, or you're under pressure anywhere and at any time.

It doesn't have to be for five minutes. It can just be for 30 seconds to 1 minute. Since you've been doing it, it'll be easy, and it works like magic. You notice a release even from the first inhale and exhale. It's an excellent stress relief therapy.

Emotional Regulation Games and Exercises for Kids

Emotional regulation is the act of identifying, understanding, and controlling one's emotions and applying them appropriately. You can also define it as being in charge of your emotions.

While it's easy for most adults to regulate their emotions, it's hard for kids. That's because their prefrontal cortex hasn't developed fully to regulate their emotions. That's why when a child is hungry, he starts crying, but when an adult is hungry, they get food to eat, or they bear it if there's no food around.

Kids therefore need external aid in learning to regulate their emotions. Luckily, there are so many fun games and exercises that can get them started. However, they will need your help, as the parent, and your involvement in playing these games or carrying out these exercises.

Here's a list of fun activities and exercises that you can engage your kids in:

- **My Feelings Game or Emojis Game:** In playing this game, you draw different expressions of emotions on paper or get emotion cards. You can also get emojis; they all serve the same function. You can then write out different emotions on different papers. Afterwards, teach them the different emotions by matching the right name tag to the right emotion. For instance, match anger to an angry face emoji/drawn emotion. Do the same for fear, confusion, happiness, sadness, etc.

- **HALT:** This is a simple way of getting your kids to define the reason for their feelings. HALT is an acronym for Hunger, Anger, Lonely, and Tired. Teach them to always remember HALT when they are in a mood and use it to define what the exact problem is so they can express themselves better. So if they're in a mood, it can either be because they're hungry, angry about something, lonely, bored, or tired. Either of these can create a feeling of discomfort and children can express it by crying, fussing, or throwing a tantrum.

- **Open Up:** You should teach your children to express their feelings in a polite manner. You can make room for this by asking them specific questions when you notice they feel upset or happy. Ask them how they feel and why they feel that way. You can also tell them how you feel when they get a chore done or when they don't. When you create an environment where they can open up and express themselves freely, it'll help quell the tantrums they throw and teach them how to address their feelings politely.

- **Freeze Dance:** This is a fun activity for the whole family. It teaches kids self-control, and the ability to listen to and follow instructions. It's simple. One person should be in charge of playing and pausing the song. So, when he plays the song, everyone starts dancing in line with the rhythm of the song (slow or fast beat). All dancers are to be conscious because the person in charge of the song can pause it at any time, and all dancers are expected to freeze once the music stops. Anyone who continues to dance is out of the game.

- **Duck Duck Goose:** This game is mainly for four or more kids. They all bow down in a circle, and one of them will be the "it". This "it" moves around the circle tapping them one by one saying "duck" at every tap, till "it" taps anyone of "its" choice and says "goose". If you're tagged as the "goose", you will chase "it" and "it" has to run till he goes back to his position and squats without getting caught. If "it" gets caught by "goose", "it" will start the process again. If he isn't caught, the "goose" becomes the next "it". This game will be very beneficial for ADHD kids as it'll teach them to wait their turn and follow instructions.

- **Playing with other kids:** It's important you teach your kids how to interact and play with other kids. You shouldn't always cocoon them indoors. Let them participate in school plays, summer camping, and other healthy outdoor activities. They'll get to build their social relationships.

These exercises and games keep them active, build their hand-eye coordination, and improve their ability to wait for their turn, listen and follow instructions, interact with others, and identify and express their emotions appropriately. This will prove to be really helpful for ADHD kids.

Recognizing Emotional Triggers: Building Self-Awareness

According to psychologist and life coach, Ana Jovanovic, "Our minds and bodies are territories for which we still need road maps. Every person has some roads they do not wish to take and some roads they feel are worth exploring. How far you'll go in your journey of understanding yourself depends on what you're ready to explore and experience" (cited by Spector, 2019).

Human composition is unique and individualistic. As our faces are different, so are our emotional responses. What upsets one person may make another feel indifferent. We all have different emotional triggers that get us to react differently.

An emotional trigger is a word, an event, or any other thing that stirs up an unpleasant feeling in you irrespective of your current mood. For instance, you're in a restaurant, drinking coffee, and chatting happily with your friends. You then look out the window, but the sight of a man squatting and tying his daughter's shoelace catches your attention. All of a sudden, you feel really sad.

That event you just witnessed may be an emotional trigger that reminded you of when your dad (who has now passed on) squatted and helped you put on your pointe for your first ballet class. This trigger brings up a sad emotion that may even draw a tear or two.

Emotional triggers feed from intense past experiences of fear, pain, happiness, anger, etc. When any of these play out again in the present or you see a similar situation, you feel those feelings creeping up inside you again. Sometimes you even notice physical discomforts or comforts like having a butterfly sensation, tight stomach, perspiration, knee knuckling, etc.

In order to recognize your emotional triggers, you need to monitor your emotions. Identify situations or words that make you react more than you should. When you identify them, you can journal about them.

Then, be sincere with yourself enough to tell yourself the truth, even if it hurts. Now think back to experiences in the past that provoked similar feelings and see if you can link these feelings up.

It may be that you dedicate your life to work and achieving more, and you're extremely upset whenever you're told you didn't do well at work. You may feel it's because you're putting in your best, but when you are honest with yourself, you'll discover it's because you're trying to prove a point to your dad, who never thought you'd make anything reasonable out of your life. That's the trigger.

When you're able to identify the root, you can then accept these feelings. If they are unpleasant, try to heal and let go. You can talk to a friend, cry it out, or talk to a professional. When you do this, the next time you see a dad helping his daughter with her shoes, you'll have a soft smile, not sadness.

After dealing with your emotional triggers and learning to manage them, you can begin to develop self-awareness. Self-awareness means keeping your emotions in check. It's seeing your emotions the way others interpret them, and not only the way you think they appear.

You may think you are in control of your emotions or that you're emotionally intelligent, but when you view your emotional displays from a third person's perspective, you'll see the defaults in your reaction.

To help in your self-awareness journey, ask your colleagues, friends, and family to define your emotional displays. With it, you'll see a new picture of yourself you never knew existed. You can begin to follow up what they say, and notice if it's true.

You can then become more self-aware of your emotions. When you feel upset or excited, be mindful of what you say or do. A lot of people make promises when they're overly happy, and when they calm down, they either forget or can't fulfill them. So, watch your reactions and responses at all times.

Teaching Empathy

Empathy is different from sympathy. A lot of people are able to express sympathy but not empathy. While sympathy is feeling pity or compassion for someone, empathy is being one with the feelings of others. It's putting yourself in their shoes and taking on their problems like they're yours. This is a skill we need to learn and teach our kids.

While some kids are innocently and ignorantly empathetic at a tender age, some others aren't. For ADHD kids, they find it difficult to be empathetic.

That's because of the emotional turmoil they go through. It's your responsibility as a parent to teach your kids how to be empathetic.

Teach them to identify and relate to the challenges of others. You can start by teaching them various emotions. To make it easier for them, do role play with them. Act like you're sad, and ask them to react when they see someone like that. You can tell them to act like they're angry, and then, you talk to them in an empathetic manner.

You can incorporate this into your daily experiences. When you see them upset or happy, try to share in their sorrow or their joy. You can even act like you're unhappy or sick and watch their reaction. Watch who will look at you and pass by; who will come to you, say sorry, and go away; and who will say sorry and lie next to you while soothing you.

In addition, you need to know that kids learn more from what they see you do, than what you say. If your actions are different from your words, they will feel confused and will easily choose to imitate your actions rather than obey your words. They watch how you talk to your spouse, the neighbor, the teacher at school, and anyone else. So, teach them both with words and actions.

Coping with ADHD-Related Anxiety

Attention deficit hyperactivity disorder is different from anxiety disorder, and someone can have one without having the other. While ADHD distorts executive functions, anxiety disorder is the extreme fear, apprehension, or unease you feel even about things that haven't happened or may likely never happen. It's different from the normal anxiety that people feel when they're about to make a presentation or enter a job interview.

However, ADHD is like a magnet for anxiety disorder. That's because ADHD distorts cognitive and executive functions, which in turn causes some shortcomings that can lead to anxiety.

A kid with ADHD may feel anxious because it's only a night until the day of the project presentation and they haven't even done much. This delay may be due to a lack of concentration or organization of thoughts caused by ADHD.

On the other hand, anxiety can worsen ADHD. In a case where an ADHD child is asked to come out in front of the class and explain a term, this may cause anxiety, which may appear as perspiration, heart pounding, and sometimes body shaking. This can in turn worsen their condition and they'll lose concentration and may even forget whatever they know.

Well, not to fear; there are solutions to this. These solutions are not a guarantee that you'll never feel afraid, uneasy, or apprehensive (all signs of anxiety) ever again. No. But they guarantee that you'll be able to cope with anxiety so you don't lose your balance at such times.

Cognitive Behavioral Therapy (CBT) is a possible therapeutic treatment for such situations. This is one of the most prescribed and effective ways of dealing with ADHD and anxiety disorder. CBT is a therapy that reconfigures your thoughts and feelings about yourself (Cherry, 2022).

A cognitive behavioral therapist will walk you through picking out your emotions about the things going on in your life at that time. They then make you analyze your thoughts:

- What do you think about yourself?
- What prompted these thoughts?
- How many of your fears have become reality?
- What are the triggers that make you feel the way you do about yourself?

They focus on your thoughts because ADHD patients always have false and irrational thoughts and beliefs about themselves. When they can't complete a task or meet the set standard, they believe they're incompetent. They always predict their next shortcomings and blame themselves for every little mistake. They think about what others think about them, and it's all negative.

Parenting ADHD with Empathy And Effectiveness

They make excuses when they do well (like it's just luck), and amplify their shortcomings. It's like they can't see anything good in themselves.

What CBT does is make them direct these thoughts and give reasons for each one. They then begin to see that one mistake doesn't define their whole lives. Their therapist teaches them to confront their fears and not ignore or accept it. He helps them see how their fears hold no water, because at the end of the day, most of them never actually happen.

CBT is a personal mind "declogger". It helps you remove the obstructions and abusive thoughts in your mind and makes you see that you're a human and have the weakness of every human -mistakes. But also helps you see and appreciate your efforts and successes.

The next solution has a lot to do with their ADHD. ADHD kids are fast and almost constant talkers. They always have something to say because their minds process a lot of information at the same time and they need to release it. This ability to hold so much information at a time can both be an advantage and a disadvantage.

It's an advantage in the sense that they can generate lots of fantastic ideas and provide quick solutions to problems. However, it's a disadvantage because it heaps ideas and tasks that may begin to seem too great and difficult to carry-out. Once they are not able to pick out these ideas to implement them one after another, they begin to feel extremely anxious.

So, teach your ADHD kid to journal their thoughts and ideas. They should then take and focus on them one by one. They can even place them according to priority. When they select a task, help them break down the process of finishing it and let them take it one after another.

One of the tasks can be apologizing to a friend whom they hurt verbally. You can help them write out what they'll say when they'll go see the person, and where, and you can role play with them before they go. This will relieve them of the stress of thinking about everything. Once they're done with a task, let them strike it out and tell them how well they've done.

Embracing Emotional Regulation

This next solution will require a parent's help. Parents are to enlighten their ADHD kids on the possibility of anxiety disorder. As a parent, you need to teach your ADHD child the symptoms of anxiety disorder, and give them instances when this can happen. Ask them if they've felt any of these symptoms and how frequent it is.

When they open up to you, you can then teach them to cope with it. You can also act it out with them. Act like you're anxious and then calm yourself by first analyzing the situation. What is true and real, and what is false and generated in the mind? When you do this, teach them to do the same.

In teaching them to calm themselves, you can introduce another solution that will help. That is breathing, mindfulness, and yoga. These are easy-to-do, yet, proven ways of coping with anxiety. So, the next time they're anxious, they can close their eyes and take deep breaths. It's an almost instant relief for anxiety.

Lastly, if their anxiety disorder is chronic, take them to see a pediatrician. They can be placed on stimulants or non-stimulants (as the case may be) if it's their ADHD that is the primary cause of their anxiety. If it's the other way around, they can be placed on other anti-anxiety medications. Whatever the medication, let it be followed by some helpful therapy.

Creating an Emotional First Aid Kit

A first aid kit is a small box that contains key medical supplies for emergencies and minor injuries. This has almost the same meaning as an emotional first aid kit. The only difference is that an emotional first aid kit is not a physical box.

An emotional first aid kit is an arsenal of aids that helps you get over emergency emotional and psychological stress and trauma. It's a soothing (although temporal) "balm" you apply once you feel you've got an emotional injury.

Parenting ADHD with Empathy And Effectiveness

Emotional injuries are one of the most painful injuries ever because they can't be seen and they affect your mind and your body. You'll notice that when you lose a dear loved one, you feel a deep hurt in your heart like someone cut you within. You lose interest in doing anything and spend your days brooding and crying.

Emotional hurts can affect our work, day-to-day operations, mood, and even our health. That's why it's important you have an emotional first aid kit (EFAK) that you can apply in hurtful situations. When it comes to EFAK, what works for one person may not work for another, and what works for one hurt may not work for another.

So, you need to arm yourself with as many as possible. One such emotional aid is food. This is one aid that works for me especially when I feel overwhelmed, upset, or seriously stressed. Food has a way of taking your pain.

It serves four functions for me. One, it receives the aggression I pass on. Two, it helps me think. Three, as I eat and think, I let go and feel relieved, or identify my emotion and either cry it out or sigh it out. Four, it soothes me from the inside. However, the aid of magic lies in eating your favorite meal or what your body craves at that point.

Another aid you should keep are good and understanding friends and family members, especially the ones with active listening skill. There are times when you feel hurt and just want to talk about it and put it all out. It can be in a case when you get dumped by your lover, or your rival in class did something spectacular that you couldn't do and you feel jealous, or you get betrayed by a close friend.

In these kinds of situations, you will feel like talking to someone and pour out your anger, resentment, or sorrow. You should have two or three people you can call or meet at such times. When you're listened to and your emotions affirmed, you'll feel a lot better and be able to interpret the situation more rationally. It also allows you to release those pent-up

Embracing Emotional Regulation

emotions so you don't hurt yourself or make a drastic decision that you'll regret later.

In addition, you can try listening to music, or a podcast, or recite a mantra or motivational quote. For some people, certain genres of music with certain lyrics serves as a balm when they're emotionally down. For some others, it can be a particular podcast that probably focuses on being calm or being your best self. Listening to this can calm them down and refocus their minds to what matters most. For others, it may be a mantra they recite every morning or every time they're hurt that reassures them of who they are.

If you're not sure of which will work for you, you can try all of them when you feel emotionally down and see which works best. You may find out it's a particular song that may do the magic and help you relax.

Again, your aid can be a soothing memory that is lodged in a photo or a teddy, or even a religious item. Keep these close by so you can use them in emergency situations. Your aid can even be to talk to, cuddle, or beat up your teddy bear depending on the emotion the situation generates in you.

Know that EFAK is mainly a temporal solution. For more permanent solutions, you need to confront the situation and address it. See where you went wrong and where the other person did. If you can let go, let go. If you can't, confront it in a rational way after probably seeking advice from someone with a clear head.

What EFAK does for you is help relieve the pain at that moment. It clears your head and mind so you can see the situation from every angle and not just the angle where you're the victim. You're then able to seek advice and follow it, or think of a better way of handling the situation. When you let out your emotions at the get-go, you'll be able to heal faster.

If you keep all that emotion in and try to bury it, all you're doing is letting it pile up. That's not a solution because one day, you'll encounter the straw that'll break the camel's back, and you'll find yourself pouring out emotions that have lingered for ages. You may end up saying some very hurtful things or making rash decisions that are extreme for the case at hand.

Takeaway Four

Kids with ADHD have a lot of challenges, one of which is emotional dysregulation. They're unable to control their emotions or think about how others feel when they let it out harshly. If not curtailed, this will not only affect them psychologically, but also socially.

As a parent, it's your responsibility to teach your kids how to regulate their emotions using practical approaches like mindfulness techniques, CBT, empathy, and emotional games and activities. As they practice with these, they'll be better able to identify and manage their emotions. This will also enhance their well-being and relationships with other people around them.

Chapter 5

Fostering Focus and Attention

Success is not final, failure is not fatal: it is the courage to continue that counts.
—**Winston Churchill**

Attention Challenges in ADHD

One of the primary symptoms of ADHD is inattention. Inattention is the inability to stay focused or listen closely to someone who is speaking. Unlike the other symptoms of ADHD—hyperactivity and impulsiveness—that are easily noticed, inattention is easy to miss.

It's hard to detect, especially, during your child's early ages, because there are loads of excuses you can substitute for it. If a 2 or 4-year-old child is easily distracted in class or can't follow instructions at home, you'd likely attribute it to childishness, or playfulness. It's mostly detected during their high school days when they are more independent and are seen as less childish. At this point, you expect them to know enough to be responsible for themselves. When you begin to notice poor academic performance, inability to complete school projects or finish assignments, and inability to obey or remember instructions at home, then you'll be able to tell that something is wrong.

When you notice these abnormalities in your child, you should visit a pediatrician for examination and confirmation if it's truly ADHD. That's because there are other factors that can be responsible for inattention. Some of these factors include:

- **Obsessive Compulsive Disorder (OCD):** It keeps a child's mind distracted most of the time. The child will have obsessive and irrational thoughts and fears about things they must do to avert the unknown danger that lives only in their minds.

- **Trauma:** Childhood trauma can also cause the mind to be distracted as unpleasant images and memories keep flashing in the child's mind.

- **Anxiety disorder:** AD can keep a child distracted because the child is always anxious about unknown events that may never happen.

However, if after a thorough medical examination, it's confirmed that your child suffers from inattentive ADHD, you need to understand some challenges your child is bound to face.

For one, they will be very disorganized. If they're grown and ashamed, they may try to hide it, but if you're sensitive enough, you'll notice it. You'll notice how their rooms are always unkept, they can't place the plates and cutleries in the right order, and they other disorderly behaviors.

Secondly, they seem forgetful. They can't remember where they kept the book they read the previous day. They can't seem to ever be able to find their shoes or socks every morning. You'll tell them to do something when they return from school but come home to see it undone because they honestly forgot ever getting any instruction. They may even remember they received an instruction but can't remember what it was exactly.

Again, they're almost always distracted. You can't get them to contribute to a discussion because their minds might have trailed off while you were talking. At school, they get distracted by a flying bird, side talk at the back of the class, someone walking past the door, and even the teacher's voice distracts them at times. They just can't stay or focus on a subject matter till the end.

The distraction can make them feel bored. So the history teacher is talking about how America was founded and the challenges the country faced at the time. The inattentive ADHD student is lost at every point and at a point loses interest in trying to follow completely. Instead, he looks outside at a bird flying, begins to paint a picture in his mind, or resolves to doodle on his note.

Furthermore, they make obvious mistakes. Since they can't focus on a task, especially one they don't have an interest in, they end up making mistakes they shouldn't make. While eating, they may get distracted and spill food on themselves. They may substitute one explanation for another in different subjects because they can't retain a line of thought.

For those who try, it may take them a whole day or even two, to finish an assignment that should naturally take 30 minutes to hour. They struggle academically especially when they have to tackle a problem alone, and may not finish writing an exam in time because of lack of concentration.

As a parent, having this knowledge about your inattentive ADHD child will help you be more patient and understand why they act the way they do. This way, you don't judge them as slothful or careless.

Creating ADHD-Friendly Environments

ADHD kids find it difficult to carry out day-to-day tasks. Sometimes they can skip something as common as brushing their teeth in the morning. They need constant reminders and assistance as they lack control of their executive functions. This is why you need to create an ADHD-friendly environment.

An ADHD-friendly environment refers to a customized or intentional setting that simplifies everyday function for ADHD kids. It helps them to be more focused and productive. You can create one at home, and talk to their teachers to help create one in school also. All of these are to make your ADHD child feel comfortable and relaxed enough to carry out tasks effectively.

At home, there are certain things you can put in place to help your ADHD child. Firstly, you can create a schedule for things they are to be involved in at home. It can be time for meals, family games, park day, study time, screen time, bedtime, etc. You should post this schedule in every part of the house that they go to or use often—on the fridge, their room door, the desk in their room, their dresser, on closet doors, in the bathroom, etc.

If possible, break the schedule down to monthly, weekly, and daily. You can set reminder alarms for them on their phones or wristwatches. This way, they know what to do and when to do it.

Again, you can organize their room in an easy way. You can label everything, segment the room, and place everything in plain sight.

So, there's a label on the cloth basket that says, "DIRTY CLOTHES". Then another label on the closet door that says, "CLEAN OR FRESH CLOTHES". You can use words that are appealing or funny to label things too.

To reduce distractions, it's best to keep their reading table away from the window in their room. If need be, create a separate study room without a bed. This will give them a reading space with no distractions.

Get containers for their pen and pencils, books, assignments, etc. Let it all be labeled boldly. This way, they can learn to be organized and place things in the right places. It'll also reduce the way they lose things due to forgetfulness. You can provide a separate basket or space for their uniforms and school utilities. This will make it easy to locate in the mornings when they want to go to school.

Another thing you should control is their screen time. It should be sparse and mostly during the day. According to the renowned psychologist, Teodora Pavkovic, screen time for ADHD kids should be shorter, " Children with ADHD appear to benefit from shorter periods of screen-based activities more frequently" (as cited by, Lindberg, 2022)

It means it's better to give them 40 mins-1 hour screen time for 6 days, than 3-4 hours per week. In addition, ensure they're not looking at a screen, for at least an hour, before bed because it can hamper their circadian rhythm. Too much screen time also impedes their cognitive and coordinative functions.

Lastly, watch their diet. Ensure they avoid sugary foods and drinks, especially before bedtime. Ration their meals so they're not overfed at night before bed. It'll make them restless and unable to sleep.

Fostering Focus and Attention

On the other hand, at school, you can liaise with their teachers to provide a friendly environment for them. For one, the teachers can sit ADHD kids in the front seat, close to the board. They should keep the kids away from the windows and doors, and ensure the class is quiet to avoid distraction and aid concentration.

Teachers should make assignments given to ADHD kids as easy to understand as possible. If it's a project, pairing them with an understanding and supportive student will also help. The project process should be broken bit by bit so it doesn't seem overwhelming for the ADHD child.

Furthermore, teachers should be loud and explicit enough when teaching for easy understanding. They can make use of fun visuals or drawings for explanations and examples. The students should be made to repeat after the teacher at intervals. It'll help the ADHD child pay attention so he/she can repeat with other students.

Lastly, instructions should be written boldly and pasted on the desk of an ADHD child. It'll keep them in check and help them curb excessive movement.

Teachers and parents should reward an ADHD child whenever they get something right or put things into the labeled boxes correctly. They lack this reward system due to a shortage of dopamine in their brain, but a physical reward can make them happy. The reward should be what they like. They should also be given breaks at intervals to play around or focus on whatever interests them. Early morning walks and evening visits to the park will also help them relax.

Mindful Practices for Enhanced Focus

One main challenge ADHD kids face is lack of concentration/focus. They can't stay on a project long enough to complete it at a go. Their minds are always busy and active but only on things that interest them.

These distractions can be caused by a lack of enthusiasm about a task, anxiety, or their environment. As natural as it is for them to get easily distracted, the fact remains that if not curtailed, can result in failure both in academics and career.

However, you can help them, as a parent, by incorporating some mindfulness practices into their day-to-day life to enhance focus. These mindfulness practices will aid concentration, reduce distraction in the mind, build a positive mindset that'll spur enthusiasm, and reduce anxiety.

There are lots of mindfulness practices that can help them in other challenging areas of their lives, but these practices are mainly to aid focus.

The first is breathing exercise. It's simple and you can do it with your ADHD kid to encourage him. It involves taking gentle deep breaths and then exhaling. They can also just sit down in a quiet place, close their eyes (or open them, but closing them aids focus), and breathe normally. The aim is to be in the present and feel the rhythm of their breath. They should focus on the pace of breathing and how their body responds to it. They don't have to try to control the pace. Just let it flow freely.

Another breathing exercise you can teach them is incorporating breathing and mindfulness in everything they do, from waking in the morning to going to sleep at night. When they wake, before they get up, they should focus on the present and 2-5 take deep breaths and exhale.

When they get up, they should make their beds and try to focus on only making the bed. To make this easy for your ADHD child, tell him to think only of ways to make the bed -how to spread the sheets, fold the blanket, arrange the dolls, etc.

The next thing they should do after making their bed is to read the day's schedule you have probably passed the previous night. They should take note of the first activity (which can be teeth brushing and bathing) and do it. While they do it, they should focus only on that activity. If their minds wander, they should call it back to that activity.

Before you drop them at school, make them recite the day's schedule and how to handle each task. It'll help them focus on the day which can reduce anxiety. They can also do more breathing exercises.

In class, the teacher can encourage them to find a point of interest in the topic of the day. They can ask questions on that area and then, the teacher can use that area as an example in talking about other areas. So the child, wanting to know more about that area, gets to listen to the whole lesson since they're intertwined.

These will help curb anxiety that may make them lose focus. It also has a way of calling their minds back to the present moment and making them think of one thing at a time. It relaxes the mind and helps it think of what is happening now and how to work on it. It's nothing fancy or time-consuming. It's easy to practice and they can do it almost anywhere and at any time necessary.

Building Concentration Skills through Play and Exploration

Concentration is an integral part of our day-to-day productivity. It's the same for adults and kids. Without concentration, projects will be left half done and targets will not be met. That's why ADHD kids who already have problems concentrating, are less productive.

They easily get bored, so to keep them concentrated on something, you have to tap into the playfulness and inquisitiveness of almost every child. Play is a great tool for improving concentration and a bait for building interest. That's because kids naturally love to play, and ADHD kids are no different. The only difference is the kind of play you want to expose them to that'll aid their concentration.

Kids are also naturally inquisitive. They're growing and still trying to understand how everything works. So little things like a butterfly perched on a flower can lock their gaze. They're easily fascinated too. You want to use this natural adventurer side of them to aid their focus.

One effective play is open play. This type of play not only gives them a variety of things to choose from, it also pins their attention on one that interests them. To aid this play, you can get them open toys. What you're looking for are toys that have no rules to play it. It can be a doll house/tea party dolls, Army toys, cars, airplane, or professions toys, like a doctor, pilot, or teacher's toy.

When they find one open play that they're fascinated about, they focus on making it work. Now, the beauty of open play is that there is no right or wrong way to play it. No rules apply, so they don't have to memorize instructions. They get to determine what is right and what is not as they play, and no one can counter their 'findings'.

As they play, they are thinking only about what's in their hands and all the different ways it'll appeal to them. They are laser-focused on leading the soldiers to war (Army toys). They can make a soldier die and resurrect to continue fighting.

They can dress the doll house as they choose and get the dolls to discuss whatever topic they like. They determine when the dolls eat and when it's time for them to sleep. They're focused on making it work and this sharpens their problem-solving skills too. After a while, when faced with a situation, they think of ways to solve it rather than throw tantrums.

Another great way to aid concentration in ADHD kids is through exploration. This is like an open play too. The only difference is that it's outdoors. The best outdoor exploration you can let your ADHD child get involved in is a place full of nature - green scenery.

Research has shown that exposing ADHD kids to nature reduces their symptoms (inattention, hyperactivity and impulsiveness). It also boosts their ability to concentrate (Hoffman, 2023).

When you expose your ADHD child to nature (it can be at the back of the house or a park with lots of green), a lot catches their attention. They learn to pay attention to their environment, noticing things that you may not even have seen like butterflies, grasshoppers, ants running on leaves, etc. They tend to be one with their environment and they're fascinated about what they discover. Every day seems like an adventure for them.

Nevertheless, always watch your child as he plays outdoors. They may unknowingly pick up something that's harmful. Or they may be overwhelmed by the number of children around and it may get them nervous.

Due to the positive impact play has on the cognitive abilities of ADHD kids, you need to create time for them to engage in constructive open play, both inside and outside the house.

The Power of Play: ADHD-Friendly Games and Activities

Play is a vital part of humans, both old and young. The only difference is that as one ages, the play changes. However, we can't remove play from the human equation because of its enormous benefits. One set of people that really benefit in a practical way are those disorders, like ADHD kids.

For these kids, play is more than just a recreational activity. It helps them face real-life challenges. Play improves their executive functions and helps them stay focused on one thing at a time. It sharpens their minds and makes them think of solutions on their own, improving their problem-solving skills.

It also boosts their hand-eye coordination and builds their strength. It can also make up for the reward system that their brains lack. You can make them do a task, using their favorite game as reward bait. It'll make them do all they can to finish the task given so they can play. Social outdoor play strengthens their resolve and social interactions.

During play, especially with other kids, they're able to make mistakes and learn to correct them. When they offend a playmate, they learn to apologize. It'll help curtail their emotional excesses as they'd want to be careful next time to not offend the person again.

Play also regulates their boisterousness and streamlines it. A hyperactive child burns a lot of energy when allowed to play for 30-40 minutes, and when he's done, he'd feel a little reluctant to move about because he lets out a chunk of that hyperactivity. Playtime is release time.

Parenting ADHD with Empathy And Effectiveness

They also release stress and anxiety when they play. As they play, their minds are at rest. They're not thinking of doing something right for someone else to judge, or what anyone thinks about them. Their minds are only focused on what they are doing.

Play makes them happier and healthier. When the mind is released from thinking and worrying and begins to do what it likes, it becomes happy and more comfortable. Play also serves as a form of exercise as they get to run around, move their bodies, etc, which keeps them healthy.

There are lots of games and fun activities ADHD kids can engage in to channel the power of play positively into their lives.

- **Gymnastics:** ADHD kids will benefit a lot from gymnastics. However, it should be a sport that is individualistic and not a team sport. They can't concentrate on a team sport (like football, volleyball, basketball, etc), because of all the rules and expectations involved. But they thrive like fish in water in individualistic sports like rope jumping, skipping, swimming, hiking, tennis, horseback riding, martial arts, etc. Since it's just themselves and the coach, the rule is simple and there is less pressure. They can fail and try again as often as they want without pulling anyone down with them.

- **Expressive Arts Therapy:** This is a fun way of letting your ADHD child explore his inner self through arts. These therapists use various kinds of art - sculpture, dance, painting, drawing, acting, singing, etc- to help ADHD children discover the way they express themselves. Some flow with acting, while others flow with painting. This also serves as a point of unwinding for these kids.

- **Board games:** These games build concentration, the ability to follow instructions and wait their turn, and other executive functions abilities. They can play alone but it's best played with someone. Some board games include Chutes and Ladders, Clue, Chess, Candy Land, Catan, Go Fish, Boggle, Simon Says, Chinese Checkers, etc.

- **Indoor adventures:** These adventures include indoor scavenger hunts, treasure hunts, picnics, tents, etc. For the hunts, you can take pictures or write a list of things in the house (your kid is familiar with) that you have hidden, and let them find it. You can leave clues for them to make it easier. Or, you can leave treasures like cookies, candies, cake, etc, around the house, and give your child a clue map to find them. Let it seem like the house is a treasure Island. It's always fun for them and it'll put their hyperactivity to good use. You can also build a tent with them inside their room with blankets and pillows. You guys can have a picnic there or snuggle and read a book or tell stories.

- **Outdoor activities:** ADHD kids also benefit from outdoor activities like picnics on the beach or green scenery, camping, and a visit to a museum or park. All of these broaden the horizons of their minds and let them see new things and gain new experiences.

- **Computer games:** Minecraft is a choice game for ADHD kids because they're left with their imagination and some resources to create a safe world. Another game is Fortnite. This epic game has three modes - Fortnite Battle Royale, Fortnite: Save the World, and Fortnite Creative. They all give your kid room to explore.

- **Traditional family games:** Playing traditional games with the whole family is both fun and a way to bond. It can be hide-and-seek, obstacle path, Head-Knees-Shoulder-Toes game, Red Light, Green Light, and board games like Matching games, Egyptian War, etc.

The Role of Exercise: Physical Activity for Cognitive Focus

We all know that one form of movement or the other is a daily pattern for humans, but exercise is different. Exercise is an intentional form of body movement, sometimes in a particular pattern, that aids the overall function of the body. The role of exercise in both the old and young cannot be underestimated.

Different exercises serve different functions. For instance, the exercises that aid muscle building are different from those that aid hip strength. The world of exercise has grown so much today that there are exercises for almost all individual parts of the body. So, it's not limited to the traditional routines, like jogging, running, or fast walking.

Exercise plays a huge role in the functionality of the systems and organs in our body, especially the circulatory system. It also builds the muscles and keeps the body fit. However, away from the popular benefits of exercise are the cognitive benefits. Researchers have found that exercise aids cognitive abilities in ADHD kids (Preiato, 2021)

ADHD kids normally find it hard engaging their executive functions, sit still, and concentrate. Exercise aids all these areas and promotes their health to the point where stimulants may not even be needed any longer. There are specific exercises to aid cognitive abilities in ADHD kids but the key is consistency and duration over the type of exercise.

It simply means whatever exercise your ADHD child finds interesting enough to engage in should be done regularly. If it can be done daily, for at least an hour, that'll help a lot., r The intentionality of the exercise doesn't matter. The most important thing is that it should be done.

Exercise for one aids the production of dopamine (neurotransmitters) in an ADHD brain. Dopamine is a neuromodulatory molecule responsible for reward and pleasure. It's often called the "feel-good" hormone. It's what gives you a sense of gratification at completing a task. This molecule is low in an ADHD brain, so they lack motivation or perseverance to do something, especially something that doesn't catch their interest.

During exercise, this "feel-good" hormone increases in the ADHD brain which improves their ability to focus and carry out tasks.

Intense exercise (aerobic or anaerobic) is good for a healthier memory. When an ADHD child engages in intense exercises, it increases the production of new neurons in the hippocampus (the brain's librarian) and causes the brain to generate new neural pathways. This keeps the memory sharp which can help kids retain and remember more. It also improves blood circulation to all parts of the brain.

Furthermore, exercise can be an avenue to release pent-up stress or hyperactivity, which fosters better coordination and lightens their mood. Instead of trying to force your child to sit still, allow him to do any exercise he likes. When he's done, he'd feel relieved and happy, because hyperactivity can sometimes be a weight on their shoulders that they just need to let down.

Here are some fun exercises you can get your ADHD child to engage in for better brain health.

- Cycling
- Skipping
- Running
- Follow an exercise video
- Dancing
- Walking in a green environment
- Playing games like tennis, golf, etc.

Technology and ADHD: Finding a Healthy Balance

Technology has come to stay and not just that, it has somehow incorporated itself in our daily lives. These days, it seems as if we can't do without one form of technology or the other. However, one technology that has almost become a part of us, especially our young ones, is the screen - smartphone, PC, Computer, TV, etc.

Screen technology has lodged itself in our hearts as it makes life a whole lot easier at the press of a button. You can quickly access any information you seek, stream videos, play music, see the current trends and happenings all over the world, play games, download ebooks, and do so many things with your smartphone and an internet connection.

How can one say no to this? It's almost impossible because every day, you'll need to use your phone for one thing or another. Our PCs and computers are similar to a phone, only with a bigger screen. It has made mathematical calculation and data analysis very easy. There are sites you can access and get all the information you need as regards a subject. With the invention of AI today, you can find sites that can even help you do your assignments.

Technology has also made communication, both professionally and socially, easy and remote. You can have a job interview, hold meetings, plan events, and exchange pleasantries with friends and families far and near all online through apps like Zoom, Google Meet, or Skype.

It's no wonder our kids can't stay away from these technologies. However, as beneficial as technology seems, it has its downsides too that can affect kids negatively. For ADHD kids, it can have a double effect on them and make life a little more difficult than it already is.

LED screens emit blue light that has the characteristics of being harmful once there's overexposure to it. A child sitting before a TV screen or staring at a phone for hours every day can lead to eye issues like teary eyes, eye pain, etc.

Aside from the impact it has on the eye, it can be worse for ADHD kids. That's because it's an invitation to the eye to stay glued to the screen. It therefore affects sleeping. ADHD kids normally find it difficult to sleep, and adding screen time worsens the case.

Lack of sleep can then heighten their lack of concentration, and discomfort throughout the day. This can cause headaches/migraines if it's consistent, and increase forgetfulness, and irritation.

That's why as a parent, it's important you regulate your ADHD child's screen time. You don't have to keep them away from it completely because it's almost impossible. If they can't get screen time at home, they'll be tempted to check a lot of other places. So, the goal is to regulate it. When it's time for them to use it, allow them to use it to the fullest (of course in viewing healthy content), so that when you want to take it back, they'll easily let go.

But to protect them, let them sit 5–6 feet away from the TV and they shouldn't keep phones close to their eyes when using it. Ages 0-3 children don't need screen time. For ages 3-12, 1 or 2 hours of screen time a day is good enough. Older kids (13+) may already have a phone and you may not be able to control them (McQueen, 2022)

So to help them, tell them the disadvantages of excessive screen time and set rules to aid them, like no screen at the dining or past bedtime. This way, you create a balance with their use of technology.

ADHD-Friendly Workspace Setup: Study and Work Habits

ADHD is indeed detected in childhood, but most of the time, it progresses to adulthood. In adulthood, hyperactivity is reduced but inattention takes over. An ADHD adult finds it difficult to concentrate on a task, forgets easily, loses things can't trace back to where it was, and gets easily distracted.

This greatly hampers their work life because, at the office, there are lots of distractions like people walking around, colleagues discussing, the sound of someone typing, etc. Tension increases when it's lunchtime and they have to socialize with their colleagues. Plus the deadlines and pressure that the work environment mounts.

Although ADHD adults have it hard, so do ADHD kids. It affects their study and work life. However, there are measures you can put in place to aid your ADHD child or spouse in becoming more productive in their study and work life. The way to do this is to set up an ADHD friendly workspace.

An ADHD- friendly workspace is an intentionally designated and designed part of the house that will serve as a study area or workspace for ADHD patients. This workspace can be a room or a part of the house. The aim is to remove every form of distraction and to make the place comfortable enough for them.

This workspace should be away from windows to avoid distraction, and everything should be labeled. It's good to use comfortable (ergonomic) chairs to aid comfort. If there's nothing you can do about distractions, then they can use headphones while studying.

The workspace shouldn't be cluttered with too many things. Working from home or at home, for ADHD adults, helps relieve the anxiety of talking to people and excessive distraction, but it also promotes laxity and has its own peculiar distractions. For instance, if you're a father, your kids may come in when you're working and that's as big a distraction as it gets.

Again, the bed is right before your eyes. You're at home, so your mind can wander to what is in the kitchen and what you can snack on. All of these are distractions. So, it's important to keep all these distractions at bay. Your wife can help you keep the kids busy while you work.

Scented candles can also aid concentration. When you get used to your workspace (for adults) or study space (for kids), it becomes your anchor point. You'll feel comfortable and find it easy to work. All of these will aid your productivity and help you meet your targets. It may still take time and you may still get distracted, but practicing mindfulness at this time will help a lot.

Takeaway Five

Kids and adults with ADHD suffer from distractions, forgetfulness, and lack of concentration. This distorts their study and work life. It makes them less productive as opposed to their neurotypical counterparts. This can cause anxiety, depression, and stress because they can't seem to focus on completing a task.

It's therefore important that you help make their lives easier by allowing them (especially kids) to play (both indoors and outdoors) games, engage in exercises, and create an ADHD- friendly learning and working environment for them.

Chapter 6

Self-Control Strategies for Daily Life

You have power over your mind - not outside events. Realize this, and you will find strength.
—**Marcus Aurelius**

In one of the greatest books to have survived different seasons clearly stated that someone who has conquered himself is stronger than a general with great military successes.

David, one of the boys I had contact with, doesn't need to confront a 9-foot giant to prove he's strong; he just had to learn how to deal with the emotional issues that come with ADHD. Oh! I can tell this young boy struggled so much. But he didn't have to learn self-control alone. He had his parents and professional support. With the commitment of all parties, David acquired the right skills, such as mindfulness and empathy, to manage his emotions. Did he conquer ADHD? Not exactly, but he's a champion in class and a lovable kid at home.

ADHD kids can do more and become better with the right support. Your kid needs you to learn the necessary skills to control their emotional excesses.

Impulse Control: A Key to Self-Management

Has someone ever crept up on you before? What was your reaction? I bet you just hit them or skipped with a shriek before realizing it was a friend. Right? Or did you do worse? Funny.

The reason you reacted that way is called impulse. Let me put it this way, it was an impulsive reaction.

Parenting ADHD with Empathy And Effectiveness

Impulse is a sudden inner urge or drive to do something unplanned. You can call it, instinct, but instinct sounds a bit formal. Impulse hits the meaning on the spot. Well, impulsive reactions are natural reactions in both humans and animals in response to sudden danger, and that's a good thing.

Imagine this: You're very tired because it was a really stressful day at work. You couldn't wait to get home to pull off your shoes and just stretch out. You're walking down the street to your house since your office is just a few blocks away. Suddenly, you heard a loud bark behind you. You quickly turned around, only to see a German shepherd loose from its owner running towards you.

At this point, what do you think will happen? I'll tell you. A strength from nowhere will come upon you, and you'll run faster than Usain Bolt till you get to your house. You won't even care to know if the dog was even chasing you in the first place.

What made you strong all of a sudden and got you running home was your impulse. So, I hope you get the picture now. Moving on, impulse is good, seeing it helps us flee danger, but it needs to be controlled. As the saying goes, What you can't control, rules over you. If you can't control your impulsive reactions, then it's a problem because it'll lead you to make the wrong decisions and take regrettable actions.

So you can say impulse is like anger. There may be a valid reason for it but if you don't control it, you'll do crazy things you never imagined you could do. An uncontrollable impulse is not being able to pause before making a decision or reacting based on an emotional thrust. This is both bad and dangerous, but it comes naturally for people with ADHD.

People with ADHD don't just have impulsiveness, they have uncontrollable impulsiveness because the prefrontal cortex that is supposed to quell or heighten any danger is faulty. So when they get an inner push to do something, there's no ability to stop themselves. I will say the worst part, and it's that their impulsiveness is dominant in adolescence.

Adolescence already has its challenges such as discovering who you are, your likes and dislikes, peer pressure and all. Adding impulsiveness to it only makes it worse. This is what makes ADHD teens dangerous, to themselves and to others. If they get angry and their impulse pushes them to run, punch the TV or anything close to them, they do it. If they're really sad or feel depressed and their impulse moves them to end their lives, they attempt it.

Without adequate knowledge and monitoring, they may pile a lot of problems behind them before they become adults, or they may not even live that long. That's why as a parent or loved one, you need to watch over them. You need the right knowledge so you can teach them and help them control their impulsiveness. It may take a long time before they get a grasp of it, but with patience and love, you can save that life.

Now, before you can teach them impulse control, first of all, you need to understand why they can't control their impulse. It's all a matter of a disorganized brain. In their brain, when the amygdala receives a signal, it can't tell the severity or intensity of the signal. Therefore, it sends the signal and transmits it in its raw and exaggerated form to the prefrontal cortex and other parts of the brain. The body is then put in a "fight or flight mode" till further investigations are made.

The prefrontal cortex (the investigator) is supposed to analyze the signal to know if it's time to fight, flee, or relax, and it also analyzes the severity of the matter at hand. Whatever it resolves, it transmits to other parts of the brain for action to be taken. But in an ADHD brain, the connection between the amygdala and the prefrontal cortex is weak, so there's no analyzing of the signal. It just transmits the signal in its severity to other parts of the brain and so the reaction is always intense. That's why they seem uncontrollably impulsive.

When you're aware of this, the next thing to do is to get them to be motivated enough to want to work on their impulsiveness, because being aware of a problem and wanting to solve it is the first step to freedom. Now, here's another task for you because motivation doesn't come easy for them since their dopamine level is lower than normal. To do this, you can first tell them and allow them to reflect on the negative things they've done due to their impulsiveness, how it affects others, and how it'll affect them in future. They need to see a need to want to change because it's hard on them that they can't help themselves. So, create motivation.

When you've made them see the need for change, then, the change can begin. You can begin by teaching them to practice mindfulness breathing exercises. Then, support it with a catchphrase. Something they can say to calm themselves when they feel "the urge". Something like:

- Silence is true wisdom's best reply.

- Close your eyes, and shut your mind for a while, for there is a tranquil land that awaits your presence.

- You don't have to control your thoughts. You just have to stop letting them control you.

Saying this every morning coupled with mindful meditation and breathing can put them in check. Also, teach them to be conscious at all times so they can tell when the impulse is about to kick in.

Next, they should avoid situations that stir them up. They should avoid the guy at school who always says hurtful things to them. They shouldn't sit close to any sharp or harmful object. If someone asks a question that they don't want to answer, they don't have to. Help them identify triggers and avoid them.

Again, they need practice, after all, Rome wasn't built in a day. You don't expect them to learn only based on what you say. You see, they know what to do and what not to do, but the ability to do it is what's lacking. So, telling them what to do will stand no chance before a real-life situation. So, practice with them at home.

You can use baits like allowing them to eat their favorite snack or taking them to the park. Whatever they like. Then, use one of their triggers and watch how they react. This practice or role-play doesn't need to be planned.

You can take them unawares just to see how much progress they're making. Set them up with their other siblings and see their reaction. But when doing this, pay close attention so they don't hurt someone.

Another way they can learn is by watching you do it. When they see how you handle the annoying neighbor whose dog always pops on your land and others in the community, they'd learn and believe in your teaching (Buzanko, 2023)

Learning how to control your impulse sets you up for self-management. You may not be able to control what others do to you, or how you initially feel about it, but you'd be able to dictate how you react to these situations.

Mindful Decision-Making: Teaching Kids to Pause and Think

Decision-making is an integral part of humans. You start making decisions from when to wake in the morning, to what you'd have for breakfast, to where you'll go, who you'll meet, and what you'll do. It's so common and important and the old and the young are laden with its burden every day.

Despite the regularity of decision-making, it's not to be taken for granted because your decisions can either make or mar you, even the seemingly little ones. For instance, if you know you're lactose intolerant but decide to take ice cream because you crave it, then you'd be ready to face the consequences.

Kids also make decisions like who to play with, and so on. However, there is impulsive decision-making. This is when you react based on your impulse at the moment without considering the other person or the consequences of your actions. This is common in kids (neurodiverse or neurotypical) because they haven't developed enough emotional stamina/intelligence to think before making a decision. This is something you need to teach your kids.

You need to teach them the act of pausing and thinking before making a decision. One very helpful way to do this is to teach them mindful decision making (MDM). Being mindful simply means living in the present. It means filling your mind with what is happening in the now, or what you're doing at the time.

This doesn't mean you won't make plans for the next day or week. It only means that you aren't constantly thinking and getting anxious over past or future events and losing focus on what's happening now. When your kids learn how to live in the present, they'll be calmer and be able to pause and think before reacting.

You can start by teaching them some mindfulness breathing and meditation techniques. You can join them to do it, just to encourage them. This will introduce them to the world of the present. As they meditate and breathe on a daily basis, watch them and test them to know their progress rate. You can even use, "Hey, pause, think, act", as a mantra for them.

Mindfulness boosts calmness, and peace of mind, relieves stress, improves concentration, and gives you a sense of well-being. With these tools at your disposal, you can then teach your kids the steps to making mindful decisions.

When faced with a stressful or temper-stirring situation:

- First of all, take in a deep breath
- Secondly, let your mind think only about the present
- Thirdly, analyze the situation and ask yourself, What do I want to do? What are the consequences of that action? Is the situation worth the consequences?

Once you've followed these three easy steps, you'll tell if your actions are good by the consequences they will procure. Then, if it's not worth it, you can walk away. If you're really anxious or angry, all you need to do is, close your eyes, take a deep breath and say the mantra, "Pause, Think, Act". You can say it over and over till you feel calm enough to talk.

Reward Systems and Positive Reinforcement

Generally, kids often see parents as "correctors", and most parents prove them right. As a parent, you want the best for your child, but a lot of other things like work, house chores, bills, and the rest keep dragging your attention. You sometimes feel you're not doing enough to raise them right.

So to compensate for that, you begin to focus on what they're doing wrong. Hoping that if you can catch them doing something wrong and correct them, you'll successfully shape them into what you feel they should be.

This also happens to adults in their workplaces. At work, they may have a boss who thinks complimenting an employee will make them relax and no longer put in the work. So, they resort to complaining and picking out their faults in a bid to keep them on their toes.

Now, simply because this method "seems" to work (because the child or adult will take correction immediately), it doesn't mean it's the best. What it actually does is that it generates tension. The adult will be under subtle pressure to always meet up, while the child who knows mistakes are a part of their lives, will be too conscious of making them. This is pressure and it can mount and lead to anger, irritation, or defiance.

A better approach to raising a child right or helping an adult do better work is the positive reinforcement and reward system. This system focuses on strengths above weaknesses. It promotes, amplifies and commends good deeds above mistakes (Tripp, 2023).

It's a reward system that you can adopt. You want to see the good your child is doing and not always the bad. If it's time to do an assignment and you found the book before them, but they're laughing and playing with their siblings, don't yell or order them to do his assignment.

Instead, acknowledge the fact that he listened and his books are out. Appreciate the fact that he's happy. Then, you can use play as bait for him. So, you will give him a time frame to finish his assignment, and if he finishes in that time, he will be allowed to play. If you check the assignment and he got it right, you can even add a treat to the play.

This is a better way of approaching the matter, and it solves so many problems. One, he still retains his smile and happy mind. Two, he is extra motivated to do his assignments. Three, you can plan to do something else with your time when he is playing. Everyone is happy.

Likewise an adult. It can be at work or even with your spouse. Acknowledge the good things they do and emphasize it. You can get gifts for them as a reward, or if it's at work, a bonus will lift the spirit and keep the employee motivated.

Setting a future reward they can look forward to will also go a long way in enforcing the right behavior. They will gladly do what you ask and even go beyond just to please you because they interpret reward for hard work as value. It means you value them and see the work they put in to be good workers or good children.

Developing Self-Control through Creative Activities

Kids are mostly full of energy and innocence and these characteristics affect the way they act and react. So it's easy for a child to throw a tantrum for not getting ice cream and stop immediately when it touches their hand. Self-control is therefore a foreign term to them.

But they need to learn it (including adults) in order to be better communicators, make reasonable decisions, improve their problem-solving skills, control their emotions, and make the right decisions. Kids are easily bored with too much talk, but they're not tired of having fun. Adults too can have a little fun.

So how about learning about self-control and having fun at it? That's why games and fun creative exercises are the best teachers. Your kids will think they're playing but they're learning important skills that begin to register in

Self-Control Strategies for Daily Life

their minds. After a while, when faced with a situation, they'll unconsciously react the way they did while playing the game.

Some fun games and exercises to help kids learn self-control include:

- **Green Light, Red Light:** This is a common game and it's fun. It's best played with other children. One of the children will be the leader, and he'll stand apart from others. He'd then call, Green Light. When he calls it, the other children can start coming towards him. But he will suddenly call out Red Light, and everyone is supposed to freeze in whatever position they are at the call. Anyone who moves before the next Green Light is called is out of the game. The leader can choose the pattern of movement to be hopping or crawling, running or walking. Whatever they agree on. It helps kids listen and obey instructions. It also develops their motor skills.

- **Body Part Mix-Up:** This is another fun exercise that will teach the kids how to pause and think before doing something. The teacher or parent or even a fellow student will stand apart as the leader. The leader then calls out, Touch your legs. Everyone touches their legs. It can be more complex, like touching your legs, eyes, and ears. To make it more complicated, the leader can tell them to touch their eyes when he says toes. So, the leader then calls out, Touch your eyes, ears and toes. The kids need to think before touching because if they rush into it, they will go for the toes since they've touched the eyes and forget that toes are eyes.

- **Role play:** This game is great because it's vast. You can tell and teach any moral lesson you choose. You can make up a short play with your kids and give them the names of the characters. It can be something simple like acting to apologize to another person. You can make up another story where one will say something hurtful and the other has to apply self-control before answering. So, you can make up anything.

- **Clap Game:** This game teaches kids to wait and listen to instructions before acting. So, the leader (can be anyone), claps in a particular pattern, and the others have to listen and clap in that same pattern. The leader can start with something simple like a three-hand clap, and then progress to more complex clap patterns. They can make it extra fun and remove anyone who doesn't get the clap right.

- **Staring contest:** This sounds odd, but it's a great way for kids to make friends, and it teaches them to be bold when they meet someone. Two kids are to stand facing each other. They are to lock eyes and no one is to laugh or shake. To make it more fun, other kids in the background can say funny things to make them laugh. The one who laughs first is out.

- **Jenga:** This is an interesting but fun game for both kids and adults. It teaches patience, improves hand-eye coordination, and reduces impulsiveness. Jenga is a tower made of 54 stacked blocks. The game is to remove blocks from the tower and place them on the top of the tower without it crumbling. As the game progresses, the tower becomes shaky. You need to be extra careful and watchful while playing this game. The person that removes or places a block that makes the tower fall, loses.

- **Musical chairs:** This is a really fun game that'll get everyone on their toes but excited. To play it, if there are 7 players, place 6 chairs in a circle (the chairs placed should be one number less than the number of players). Now, you'll play a song and they should dance round the chair. You can then suddenly pause the song. Once the song stops, they are to sit on the chairs placed. The last person standing is out. When one person is out, remove one chair. Continue till you have a winner. This helps kids and adults stay conscious in the present, and act positively on impulse.

- **Connect Four:** This is a two-player game that improves focus and problem-solving skills through critical thinking and patience. The game involves colored disks and a vertical grid. Each child is to choose one color of the disk. They are to take turns in placing the disk on the vertical grid. The goal is to place your colored disk four in a roll, vertically, diagonally, or horizontally. So, you're both trying to block each other's disks while still trying to connect your four disks.

- **Hide and Seek:** This is a common but really fun game. The best part is that it's for both kids and adults and can be played even at school. One player will close his eyes and count to a certain number. This will give other players time to hide. After counting, the seeker will have to go in search of the players. They need to be intentional about their search and think of places someone would hide. The first person he finds becomes the next seeker.

Self-Monitoring: Tracking Progress and Behavior

As humans, we're not perfect in character and behavior. Even adults lose it sometimes and it's understandable. I mean, there are lots of things that can push you out of character. There is work stress, a family to take care of, trying to hit a set target, fulfilling your dream, bullies at school, and decisions to make every day.

Continuous exposure to some of these stress-related duties can even make you develop a character that is not natural. For example, a single mother who just lost her husband now works three jobs just to take care of her four children. Her two boys are not doing well at the school she could afford and are not even trying. One of her girls has ADHD, and the other girl is trying to help her mother as much as she can while still in school.

A woman like this, who probably was known to be very calm and always happy when her husband was alive, may suddenly become paranoid, aggressive, and sad. There will always be something to yell about. She may develop these behavioral patterns because life happened and stress increased.

Let's assume a related scenario for a child. Let's say the child is caring, sympathetic, and always willing to help others. But one day, the child is hurt and needs help, but is abandoned by everyone and laughed at. This child can feel really hurt within and begin to care less because they feel no one cares about them. They might become withdrawn or reckless. Life happened.

So, lots of things can happen to change our behavior or make us act out of line. For people with ADHD, their natural symptoms of hyperactivity, impulsiveness, and inattention is already a behavioral defect.

However, the good news is that there's a way to work on any unpleasant behavior you portray. The tool for this is called self-monitoring. Self-monitoring simply put is, being your personal police officer. It's the tool that helps you keep your behavior, emotions, and lifestyle in check with a set standard.

To begin your self-monitoring journey [kids (with ADHD or not) and adults alike], you need to first acknowledge you have a problem. You see, this is seemingly the most difficult step. That's because it's easy to give excuses for a bad habit or behavior. No one wants to admit that they're bad or are not perfect even when it's so obvious. But if you can't admit that there's a problem, you won't be able to solve it because you can't solve a problem that doesn't exist.

If you're willing to know if there's a problem, then, start by asking those closest to you, especially those you're living with. Ask them to tell you things about yourself that they think you should change. You may be shocked by what you hear.

Secondly, listen to what people complain about the most. It's true no one is perfect but there are some negative attitudes that are generally accepted as being negative. For example, if you're quick to jump into a fight, or you easily abuse and insult people, then that's a problem.

For ADHD kids, not being able to wait in line for their turn, answering questions before it's even completely asked, losing things, and emotional overreaction can be a problem. It may be natural to them but it still doesn't make it good.

At home, if your spouse is always complaining that you're a nagging spouse, listen to those things. That's how you identify the problem.

The second step to self-monitoring is picking out a problem to monitor. You can make a list of all the negatives you would like to change in your life. Now, it doesn't even have to be something so harsh. It can simply be that you want to stop eating junk food, or you don't want to be a wasteful spender anymore. In making the list, write them in order of priority.

The third step is to draft a scoring sheet, and set daily goals. You can break your daily goals down per hour. So the aim is to either give yourself a score or tick the box each hour you stay through without performing that negative act. At the end of the day, check your progress for the day and see if you faulted. At the end of the week and month, collate your progress (Sippl, 2023).

Having an accountability partner or a coach will help here. It can help keep you in check if you know you have to report to someone to get their approval or disapproval. However, another self-motivator outside having an accountability partner is a personal reinforcement. Set short-term and long-term rewards for yourself.

If you can't control the reward, give it to someone to keep it for you. You can only collect it when your boxes are ticked off. That'll motivate you to do better. Nevertheless, keep your eyes on the real price which is the satisfaction of developing a positive attitude.

Furthermore, you don't only have to set goals for changing negative behavior. You can make a goal to improve on a positive one. You can also encourage your child to do the same. It's easier to improve on positive behavior and get rewarded for it than trying to stop a negative one. In the long run, the positive one will overshadow the negative and curb it.

Goal Setting for Kids: Achievable Milestones

Goal setting is not only for adults, kids also need to learn this important skill which will help them when they grow up. Goals are set targets with a time limit that one consciously tries to meet up with. Goals can be long-term or short-term.

Setting goals is important because it gives the child direction and helps them achieve tasks. It's especially helpful for ADHD kids who struggle to finish tasks. When they are able to set a goal and tick it off their list, they feel happy and relevant. They feel like they've accomplished a lot. It can be a great boost for their academic performance and other areas of their daily lives (R, 2019).

There are different types of goals kids can set.

- **Social goals:** It involves their social interactions. They can set goals on making new friends, strengthening relationships, etc.

- **Academic goals:** It involves setting goals to improve academic performance on various subjects. It can also be a goal to perform better in extracurricular activities at school.

- **Attitude goals:** This is a goal to improve on a positive attitude or manage a negative one. ADHD kids will benefit from this.

- **Home goals:** Kids can set goals on how to do house chores, arrange their rooms, etc.

However, they need your help as their parents to advise, direct, and monitor their goals. Here's how to help your kids set goals.

- **Get your kid interested in goal setting:** The first and most important step in a kid's goal setting is interest. Kids are more interested in play and fun activities than in carrying out a task. However, there's an innate nature in every man, kid or not, that wants to feel useful. There's a satisfaction and joy that comes from achieving something tangible. This should be your tool. You need to get kids to understand the need to set a goal and the benefits of actually seeing one through. You can set rewards for them as extra motivation. But they need to see a reason to do it, otherwise, they won't be able to see it through. They may also do it for a while and stop without motivation, and that will hinder the main purpose of goal setting. While their goal is to complete a task, yours is to ensure they imbibe the act as a lifestyle. You need them to do it to the point where you don't even have to tell them to or give a reward.

- **Guide them to choose goals to set:** This is also important. Guide your child to choose areas where he needs to improve, develop, or reduce. If you have an ADHD child, getting them to put things in the appropriately labeled container in their rooms can be a goal. Getting them to study other subjects aside from the one they like can be another. Guide them to see areas they need to work on or areas they need to improve and the reasons for doing it. Then you can add a reward for extra motivation.

- **Set SMART goals:** In teaching kids to set goals, ensure the goals are SMART, that is, Specific, Measurable, Achievable, Relevant, and Time-bound. SMART goals shouldn't be porous or vague. The goal shouldn't be to, Do House Chores. That's a vague goal. A specific goal is, *arranging my clothes in my closet every day*. Or, *washing the plates after dinner*. Or, *study math from 4-5pm every day*. That's specific and measurable. The goals also need to be achievable, that is goals like getting an A in English or Starting a friendly conversation with a classmate. An unrealistic goal is an ADHD child wanting to make 20 friends in two days. It sounds nice but it's nearly impossible and it'll be overwhelming for them. Again, goals are not goals if they're not time-bound. They should be set to be accomplished at a particular time so they can be useful. For instance, a child cannot set a goal to join the basketball team a week before the end of the term and expect to play in the finals. It's impossible and time will not let the goal be useful.

- **Break the goals:** ADHD kids can get overwhelmed when they're faced with too many goals to achieve. So, teach them to take it one at a time. Break down the process of each goal so they can follow it step by step. This will make them eager to complete the task and it'll reduce anxiety.

- **Monitor your child's goal:** You can do this by making a daily to-do list for them that they should tick off. So, the steps to completing a goal can span for a week, and have 5 steps. They are to tick each step off after completing it. So at the end of the week, they can tick the task off as complete and get their reward. You can monitor their list and advise them on how to go about it till they have completed each task.

Coping with Frustration and Anger: Emotional Regulation Techniques

Emotions are a part of life. Even animals express emotions. When you travel for long and return, your dog will rush in excitement to meet you. That's emotion. Emotions can be negative or positive. Positive emotions are excitement, love, etc, while negative emotions are sadness, anger, frustration, depression, etc.

Now, different people respond differently to negative feelings like anger and frustration, and you'll agree with me that there are lots of issues in life that can lead to frustration. However, just because you feel angry or frustrated, it doesn't mean you always have to react negatively.

You need to learn how to control your temper and cope with frustrating events so it doesn't affect you negatively or those around you. The tool you need is emotional regulation techniques. Emotional regulation techniques are various practices you can adopt that will enable you to understand your triggers, and control, and manage your emotions.

There are people with high emotional intelligence who not only know how to manage their emotions, but can also predict how their reactions will affect another person. They can also predict the emotions of others, and the possible causes and how to treat them. They are active listeners and always have a soothing and wise word to give.

When you have such a friend, you find it easy to talk to them. Well, you can be that friend if you can practice one or more of the following emotional regulation techniques.

Self-Control Strategies for Daily Life

- **Cognitive Behavioural Therapy (CBT):** CBT is a self-therapy that makes you think about your thoughts in the present. You learn to understand yourself, why you act the way you do, and if those actions turn out good or bad. When you're angry, take a moment to pause and think about the thoughts going on in your mind at that moment. Try to see the reason for the anger from different perspectives. Then you think of where you're at fault, and the right way to handle the situation. The right way, and the way you feel it should be handled are two different things. If someone insults you, you will want to say something, just a sentence probably, that will hurt the person so much more. But that's not the right way to handle the situation. The right way is to know the reason for the abuse and walk away if it's not reasonable enough, or address the issue. So, the right way may not always be your way, that's why you need to pause and think.

- **Emotional support:** If you're the type that easily gets angry or frustrated about things, then you need to build an emotional support wall around you. An emotional support system can be a friend who you feel comfortable sharing your feelings with, or your spouse, or a favorite teddy or a place you like to visit. An emotional support can even be standing by the beach or swimming to burn off the anger. It's something you can do that can help you release the anger or frustration. Or someone you can talk to.

- **Identify Triggers:** You need to know yourself. Self-awareness is important. It's knowing what triggers your temper, or what makes you feel frustrated. For ADHD people, frustration may come as a result of pressure to hit a target, or a a pile of workload. For you, it can even be a memory that triggers your temper. You need to identify and avoid these triggers. If your trigger is unavoidable like family, then, ensure you have a kind of emotional support system close by where you can pour out all that emotion.

- **Practice Mindfulness:** Mindfulness is a technique that cannot be overemphasized. It's so important as it keeps your mind in the present and helps you calm down. When you're upset or frustrated, your emotions build and you get an urge to do or say hurtful things. Practicing mindful thinking, meditation, and breathing will help put your emotions in check.

- **Walk Away:** This is one of the most proposed ways of dealing with anger and frustration. When you're angry or frustrated, just walk away. If it's a person you're angry with, give the person some space. If it's a task that you're finding hard to do that's causing it, leave the task for a while. You can take a walk, go have a meal, or just sleep. Don't think about the anger or frustration, just sleep. Some people recommend shouting at the sea or an open place to release the tension inside. It works too. But the aim is, don't respond to your emotions at that point. When you walk away, you feel relieved of that emotion. That's when you can start thinking of ways to handle it.

- **Adaptability:** It's easy to walk away from a friend who pisses you off, but what if it's your neighbors, or spouse, or boss at the office. You can't walk away from that. So, one way you can cope is to adapt. Configure your mind to who keeps getting on your last nerve so it can be prepared whenever the person comes around. So, if you already know that your boss always has something negative to say to you every morning, and you're his personal assistant, let your mind adapt. So when your boss comes and makes a negative comment, just think, "that's how he talks". It disables your mind from taking his comments personally anymore.

- **Self-compassion:** When you feel overwhelmed, then it's time to think about yourself. You need to create time for yourself, time to find your own happiness. If the pressure is at work, then, plan to go for a spa treatment, or the beach, or to see family during the weekend. Do something that makes you happy and keeps you in the moment. Go where it seems like all your troubles disappear. You owe yourself that much.

Anger and frustration are negative feelings that affect your mood, productivity, and even your health. That's why you need to learn to regulate your emotions so you can be happy and healthy.

Teaching Delayed Gratification: Patience and Persistence

Patience, they say, is a virtue. The world is moving on fast and everyone wants to go along with it. Kids face pressure at school to be at the top of their class or "fit" into the regimented system. Adults face the pressure of being successful like their mates and achieving their dreams. Everyone seems to be moving too fast and patience is ebbing out.

Today, when people want something, they look for the easiest way to get it. A lot of people, especially young people, no longer have enough patience to go through the process. For some others who decide to go through the process of getting something, they are not persistent enough. They start and stop halfway.

Patience and persistence are the midwives of the success we all desire, but they are not cheap virtues. You need to learn and practice till they become a part of you. It may take time, but it's worth it. Imagine a young man, fresh out of college, seeking a high-paying job. When he gets a job at a supermarket, he's impatient. He stays for two months and is out because it's not high paying enough. He keeps getting and leaving jobs. Tell me, how can such a man get the big jobs he seeks?

Everyone needs to begin from somewhere. Even if he gets the job, how will he manage it seeing that he has no prior experience? Starting small doesn't mean you're small. They serve a higher purpose and that is making you responsible. If you can keep a small job, you can keep a big one. It's all about patience and persistence.

This impatient attitude is fast creeping into the lives of our kids too. They're impatient to read. When they manage to fail once or twice, they give up. They say, practice is what makes perfect. However, a little motivation can help you develop these soft skills.

One such motivation is delayed gratification. Delayed gratification simply means delaying a reward. Or, reaping in future what you planted today. It's like starting to save for a pension at an early age. You're investing money and you're not getting the returns instantly for use today, but you keep investing because you know one day, you'll enjoy it more than if you got it today.

Some people prefer instant gratification to delayed gratification. It's those people who tell you to eat what you have today and let tomorrow worry about itself. That sounds reasonable but eating everything you have today isn't reasonable at all because rainy days will surely come.

You can liken it to taking time and energy to plant an orange seed today, so you can have a whole tree of oranges in the near future. Delayed gratification doesn't mean you save all you have for tomorrow. The motto for delayed gratification is, Eat Some, Save Some.

In order to do this, here are some steps you can follow:

- **Have a plan:** You need to have a workable plan. Your plan should include the thing you're saving for in the future, why you're saving it, and how to go about it. For instance, let's say you're 20 years old, and you want to start saving for your pension. Your pension plan should include where you'd get the money. If it's your current salary, then what percentage will you set aside every month for this investment plan? The next thing is which custodian will you go for, and then, when to start. At the end, you write why.

- **Patience, Persistence, and Discipline**: You need to be disciplined enough to remove the said percentage every month. To help you, if you earn $300 monthly, and you want to remove $100, just configure your mind to think that you earn only $200 monthly. This way, all your plans have to fit into that amount and you can easily remove the percentage. If you're not that disciplined, then your bank should do the transfer for you monthly. So, once your salary is paid, your bank automatically transfers $100 to your pension account. You also need to be patient and persistent to achieve your goal. Know that it may not always be a bed of roses, so that when you meet the thorns, you won't give up.

- **Keep your eyes on the price:** I'll use myself as an example here. If I get a really tasking job, the first thing I do is to calculate how much it'll pay. The money becomes my motivation. So when I get tired or feel overwhelmed, I remember the money I'll get at the end and I'll continue. So, when you start a long-term plan, keep your eyes on the day you'll eat the fruit of your labor. When you feel you should stop investing in a pension, or reduce the money, think of how it'll affect you in future. Then imagine when you're 50, 65, or 70 years of age, and you want to retire. Imagine withdrawing a huge amount of money that can serve almost any purpose you may want at that time. You can even calculate the return you'd get at the end. This should spur you to keep on.

- **Believe in yourself:** You need to keep faith alive. Surround yourself with people who believe in you and will always have your back, so that when you feel discouraged, they can hold you up. No one said it would be easy, and no one ever became successful by giving up on their dreams. You need to keep pushing and believe in yourself and what you're doing. It will work because it has to.

Takeaway Six

Self-control is key for everyone, ADHD or not, kids and adults alike. It's important for making reasonable decisions, controlling your emotions, and being calm, and productive in life. It is also important in building and strengthening relationships. Self-control is a skill that can be built through self-awareness and behavioral skills such as patience and perseverance. One of the emphases of this chapter is that these skills can be learned.

Chapter 7

Time Management and Organization

Don't count every hour in the day. Make every hour in the day count.
—**Alfred Binet**

Time Mismanagement: Strategies for Punctuality

Peter and Tess *were* interns in the same company. Peter always arriv*ed* at the office every day, at least 15 minutes before the official hour. Tess on the other hand, will always arrive 15-30 minutes after the official hour. When their boss call*ed* for them in the morning, Tess w*ould* either not be around, or will be seen running in at that moment.

After three months, the company had a vacancy and decided to promote an intern. Though Tess was a more productive employee than Peter, their boss chose Peter for the promotion.

Life is measured in time. Without time, nothing happens. That's why you shouldn't joke about it. Punctuality is one soft skill that everyone appreciates because it saves time, and tells a lot about one's personality. Imagine having a test at school and getting to school 30 minutes or an hour after the test has started. You'll likely fail that test.

Time management is the ability to plan and use time appropriately to achieve set goals. Time mismanagement, on the other hand, means being irresponsible with time. It's like planning to go grocery shopping on your way from work because there's no food at home, but instead, you follow a colleague to a party you just heard of at work.

Time Management and Organization

Time mismanagement is wasting time. You may have planned to plant some flowers, and you do plant them but you spend the whole day on that one activity. Why? Because as you plant, you stop to eat, take and make calls, go on social media, talk with a neighbor about the latest news, and then rest. All of these are distractions you could have avoided to finish planting the flowers in time.

No one wants to do business with a time-waster because time is precious. Both kids and adults need to learn the importance of punctuality. Punctuality means you value time, yours and others. It means you're responsible and serious about the task at hand or your job. It sets you up to be more productive and hit your daily targets. It also makes others feel happy when you're on time for a birthday party, family dinner, etc.

However, some people can't help being late no matter the amount of time they have to get ready. If you're finding it difficult to manage your time, here are some strategies you can adopt.

Firstly, plan your day ahead. You can plan for the next day or the previous night. You can do this by making a priority to-do list for the next day, or just map out a mental picture of something you don't have the strength to write (though I'll always recommend writing it out).

Now, making a list is one thing, following it up is another. So, on the list, draw your map for the day. It doesn't have to be anything fancy. What I mean is this: let's say your plan is to go to work, get groceries, visit grandma to give her her medications, and then pick up the kids from school. Now, think of the routes you will take to get to these places. If grandma's place falls on the route to your office but the grocery shop is off that route, then, go to grandma's place from the office. Then, you can go pick up the kids so you don't keep them waiting after school, go grocery shopping, and then head home. That saves you time.

Another time-saving strategy is, to stay on track. Never go off course except in the case of an emergency. If you've made a plan for the day, don't change it because a friend asks you to accompany her somewhere or something less important comes up. Whatever should make you change your plan should be much more important than your plan.

But having a plan doesn't mean you can't meet with friends or do other things, so, when making your plan, leave gaps. In those hours when you're free, you can do other things. Your plan is not necessarily everything you'd do in a day like bathing, brushing, eating, and taking calls. If you can do that, perfect, but if not, just lose out on the key things you must do before the end of the day, and allocate the time to do them.

Moving on, another time saver is delegation. This is very important, and it simply means you don't have to do everything yourself. If your to-do list is full, look out for those things you can assign to others and tell them to help you do it. For instance, if you have grown kids at home, you can assign chores to them, so you don't have to return from work and start doing chores. You need time for yourself too.

If you have a friend who's going to get groceries, you can give the person money and ask the person to get it for you too. At work, if you have assistants or team members, assign the task at hand to them. Break the project into bits so everyone will have a share of it. Learn to delegate duties. It gives you time to do other things.

Finally, review your to-do list at the end of each day. It'll help you keep track of your time management skill progress. You'd know what you had to put away where to reschedule it, and what you have to do the next day.

Time mismanagement reduces pressure and anxiety because you're always meeting up on your work, and doing what needs to be done (Pinnix, 2023).

Organizational Skills for ADHD Kids

One thing ADHD kids find very challenging is being organized. It's like a farfetched ability because their brain configuration cannot understand how neurotypicals do it. That's because they lack executive functions.

Time Management and Organization

An ADHD child's room will always be scattered, and at school, their lockers are scattered. This is why they easily lose things and because they didn't think before keeping it, they aren't able to remember where they kept it. They just do things as they feel, and can't pick up after themselves.

Punishment at school or at home will do no good for ADHD kids. It'll only worsen the case. Punishing them when they know that they can't help themselves will make them feel small, and lazy, and think something is wrong with them. This kind of mindset can mess up other aspects of their lives because what others think about you cannot affect you as much as what you think about yourself.

This is why you need to teach your ADHD child organizational skills. Organizational skills provide them with the best strategies to organize their properties. There are a number of ways to make organization easy for ADHD kids.

The first is to provide the necessary things they need. To make it easy for them to organize, set laundry baskets and containers for different things in their rooms and label them. The container for pens and pencils, the one for science and another for art subjects, the one for assignments, etc. In the house, put things separately so they can easily find it and put it back. Let the plates be in one place, the cups in another place, and so on. This way, when they remove something, with the label you've put, they'll know where to drop it.

Secondly, teach them early preparation. They should prepare for the next day the night before. So, they should lay out their uniforms, socks, shoes, books, etc. Then you will inspect it. They should always prepare before any event they want to attend. It'll make it easy to find everything they need in the morning without wasting time.

Thirdly, set a daily routine or to-do list for them. You can write it on a sticky note and stick it to the books they'll be using at school that day. This plan will help them remember what they should do and when it should be done.

Lastly, set a routine for your ADHD child. They need something stable and hard to forget. So, set a morning routine, weekend routine, night routine, meal routine, etc. You can paste the night routine on the bathroom door. So they know they have to brush, bathe, change into their pajamas, drop the dirty cloth in the dirt basket(already labeled), arrange all they'll need for the next day, and then turn off the light, and sleep. Other routines should be detailed - what you expect them to do and what they shouldn't do.

The key to achieving your goal of inculcating organizational skills into your ADHD child as a parent is patience and love. There may be times when it seems like they haven't learned anything after you've tried to show them for months. You need to be patient and correct them in love.

If you have a child who refuses to learn then use tough love on that child. Tell him that if he loses anything, you won't cover up for him again, and he'll pay for whatever he spoils or loses. When you say it, do it. When you do it once or twice, remind them how things can get better only if they learn to be organized.

However, you should always have a backup plan. They're still your kids, so you need to temper justice with mercy. For one, have duplicates of their important documents, and provide extra notes and pens/pencils for them. Also, have two or three extra uniforms hidden somewhere in case of emergency.

Mindful Planning Techniques: Routines and Schedules

Going through the day and meeting up with tasks and deadlines can be very stressful and difficult for people with ADHD. The fact that they are unorganized, forgetful and make unnecessary mistakes compounds the problem. But this doesn't mean they have to go through every day frustrated with unfinished projects.

Mindful planning is just the tool they need to make their days stress-free and productive. Whether they're a working adult or a school kid, mindful planning will help them stay on track and help them achieve more every day. Mindful planning involves planning tasks based on their importance and/or urgency. You're able to schedule your time and set routines that will make life easier.

To practice mindful planning, you can start by listing all you need to do. This will help you in creating a schedule. You should make this list in one place (a pocket notebook, your smartphone, etc). Preferably, something you can carry around. So, whenever you identify something you need to do, or someone asks you to do something for them, immediately write it down. This way, you can't forget.

The next thing you can do is to make a schedule, daily. A schedule is a list of daily tasks with time allocated to each task. To make this schedule, you can adopt the Eisenhower Matrix planning strategy. It has four parts and you're to plan your daily tasks this way. The first one is Do. Under this, you'll list the tasks that are both important and urgent. To identify it, ask yourself, What will go wrong today if I don't do this? If something will, then it's a Do.

The second is Schedule. Under it, list tasks that are important but not urgent and plan a time to do them. To know this kind of task, ask yourself the same question as at first. But this time, the answer should be that nothing will go wrong but it's better it's done today.

The third is Delegate. Here, list urgent tasks that are not important, then assign them to people who can help you do them. These are tasks that need to be done but you don't necessarily have to be the one to do it. Lastly, Delete. Select and remove tasks that are neither important nor urgent. Or if you still have time, you can list them as the last things to do (Victorino, 2020).

Another mindful planning technique is segmentation. ADHD makes your mind feel overwhelmed when it's faced with a huge task. So, whether it's a school project or an office project, you want to segment it. What do you do first, and what can come after? Break down your tasks into what you can do in 20-30 minutes. Don't try to finish everything in maybe 4-5 hours. As you break your task, tick it off when you meet your target time, then go for a short break from time to time so you don't feel overwhelmed. This will help you finish the task even before you know it

In your schedule, don't forget to schedule for today. Don't add things you can do way later to your plan today. Remember, it's mindful planning. That's why you can't do without a schedule.

The last planning technique you can use is daily review and accountability. You want to review your schedule at the end of each day. What were you able to do? What is left? Were the delegated tasks completed? What can you move to the next day and how important is it? You do a review so you can know your progress level.

Another thing you can do to meet up with some important but not urgent tasks is to create a routine. So you know you need to do chores, and see friends and family, so create a fixed schedule for it. You can visit family every Saturday evening from 5-9 pm, and wash the dishes every day before bed. When you create a routine for certain things, it reduces the stress of thinking about how to do them. After a while, they become a part of you.

If you have ADHD and easily get distracted, you can set a reminder. You can set it on your wristwatch or phone, but it should be something you can move around with. If you're supposed to finish reviewing a report and the allotted time is 4

These techniques may not stick the first time you start doing it, so, give room for mistakes and failure. The key is consistency and persistence. If you don't meet up today, try again tomorrow. Analyze why you didn't meet up today and try to work on that tomorrow. This circle can continue as long as you see progress. It gets better after a while.

Interactive Worksheets for Time Management

It's easy to talk about time management but it's in practicing it that you can have meaningful results. Having an interactive time management worksheet for school or work is a more practical way of managing your time. An interactive time management worksheet is a worksheet that has a list of questions on how you spend your time, and a template for time management.

Why do I need one? In order to manage time, you first need to know how you use it. How many hours do you spend on each activity you do every day? How many hours for sleep, family, friends, school/work, study, play, etc.? You will then fix these details in a table. This way, you will know how long you spend on each activity, which one to spend less time on, and which to spend more time on.

An interactive time management worksheet is in the form of a questionnaire. The questions are about the way you use time each day, your work/school, and some of your characteristics. After filling out the form, you'll be able to rate your productivity level and why it's at that level. What you now need to do is to make necessary adjustments to take on more profitable tasks than non-profitable ones.

It then gives you tips on how to plan your time henceforth on a time management worksheet. This worksheet is a more practical way of keeping track of your time, activities, deadlines, and progress level. It aids you in your work-life balance and makes you more productive each day.

You feel conscious and in control of time and that reduces pressure and mental stress. Use it and start managing your time today (Feyoh, 2023).

The Power of Checklists: Daily and Weekly Planning

Have you ever forgotten an item you planned to travel with? Or have you ever forgotten to see your mom who you promised to visit? Well, that's because you didn't have a checklist. I know you have a schedule, but that's different from a checklist.

A schedule is a list of to-dos (daily, weekly, or monthly) with a timeframe (minutes, hours, or days) for each task. A checklist however is a list of activities written in order of importance that needs to be done but without a time frame. For instance, when you want to travel, you can make a list of all you need to travel with. You can then cross off each item you pack on the checklist till you're done packing. It's different from knowing that you're to travel by 6pm that day.

Each item on your checklist can also be expanded to have sub-checklists. Here's an example to clarify the difference between a schedule and a checklist with sub or mini checklists.

1. **Day's Schedule**

   - Send an Email - 8am-8:30am
   - Review a report - 9am-10:30am
   - Board meeting - 11am-1pm
   - Grocery shopping - 5pm-6pm

2. **Checklist with sub-checklists**

   - Send an Email: Particular email to send, where to find it (or are you to write it then), who to send it to and their email address, and get coffee.
   - Grocery shopping: list of things to get, where to get exactly what you want, and payment method.

This is an example of what a schedule and a checklist look like. Your checklist can extend to what isn't even in your schedule. The sub-checklists are things you need to get that task done or ways to do it. For example:

Dora's Week's Checklist.

- Pay Debbie a visit
- Call grandma
- Talk to my boss about a raise

Time Management and Organization

- Offer volunteer services

- Send a bulk SMS

- Read at least 3 chapters of a book

- Plan for a vacation

A checklist can be made for various purposes. You can make a professional checklist, like the first example I gave, a chore checklist, or an academic checklist. You can make a checklist for whatever you want to do and the power of a daily or weekly checklist cannot be underestimated. It is so important. Here are some reasons for this assertion.

First, a checklist is a powerful tool that clarifies your daily tasks. With a checklist, you know what you must do every day and how to go about it. It also serves as a kind of memory and this is very helpful for people with ADHD who are forgetful and disorganized. A checklist organizes your day and makes you plan your time, routes, and money.

If on your checklist you need to go grocery shopping and you want to do that with cash, you'll know how much to leave the house with. When you get to work and you feel like eating something, you'd know not to use the money unless you brought extra, so you can get everything on your list. So, your day's task is clear.

Again, a checklist makes you more efficient and productive. You do what you must do each day thereby becoming more productive. Without a checklist, you may want to send an important business email to a company but forget where you saved the company's email address. Or, you may forget to submit the minutes of a previous meeting because you got engaged in doing other things.

A checklist reminds you of what's important and keeps you on track. It keeps you focused on what you have to do, and if close to the end of the day, some things haven't been crossed off yet, you're able to plan how to carry them out. So, it informs and directs your daily decisions. With a checklist, you don't allow yourself to get distracted and you're able to plan your routes in order to meet up with everything on your list.

The checklist also guarantees continuous productivity. You may have some recurring tasks on your daily or weekly checklist. So you stay productive every day as you tick off that task. At a point, you'll get used to doing it and get better at it too.

So, you can make a daily or weekly checklist - things you need to do before the day or week runs out. Knowing why it's important to do it will spur you. So, close to the end of the week, if you haven't crossed off 90% of the things in your checklist, then you need to put in more effort to finish it up.

The good thing about a checklist is that the time to do it is flexible. The only boundary it has is the final date. So, if you have a week's checklist, there's no date or time attached that each task must be done, so you can do it in your free time. The only thing is that you need to complete every task before the end of the week.

This way, you're not under any pressure to complete a task in one hour or more. You're in control of your work and in charge of your day. It makes it easy for you to complete tasks and track your progress.

ADHD-Friendly Technology Apps: Digital Organization Tools

The world has experienced a lot of positivity ever since the invention of technology. As technology continues to advance, it has stretched into various areas with the aim of producing easy, fast, and efficient results. One such area is the world of ADHD.

Before now, people with ADHD went by with manual ways of staying organized. These manual ways included lots of instructions and trial and error. But today, ADHD-friendly technological tools that aid organizational skills abound. They're easy to use and highly effective.

Time Management and Organization

These tools are as simple as apps on your phone. They help people with ADHD (especially adults) stay focused on their tasks, keep a working schedule, set daily achievable goals, provide reminders, and keep track of their daily productivity progress.

Here are 7 amazing ADHD-friendly technological tools that aid optimal organization:

- **Tile App:** ADHD patients are very forgetful and it makes them lose things in the process. When they lose something, they can't remember where they kept it and since they are often disorganized, it's difficult to find what was lost, but the tile app is here for the rescue. A tile is a small amazing tracker. It's as small as a sticker and can be attached to your keys, phone, speaker, PC, etc. When you miss any of your items with a tile tracker on it, you just need to open the Tile App on your phone, locate the item, and tap "Find". It rings an alarm to indicate where the missing item is. The tile app can show you the last location where you had a missing item. It also has a network that allows anyone around your environment with the tile app to look for your item that is missing and is not nearby. You can even connect it to a smart speaker. So when you lose something, you can simply use voice command to ask Alexa to find the item.

- **Due App:** Due is a persistent reminder app which is exactly what an ADHD adult needs. You can set timers for different activities, switch activities, or put it off to a later time on this app. When it's time for an activity, the alarm goes off, and it's in auto snooze. The alarm rings and stops but continues like that till you mark off that activity as done, move it, or turn off the auto snooze. It also reminds you of tasks that have been left undone at the time it was supposed to. So this app keeps you on track and helps you manage your time and tasks.

- **Remember the Milk:** This is a task organizational app. You can write out your schedule in order of priority, add locations (and save commonly used ones), edit your schedule, add new tasks, move tasks to a later date, and keep track of your time. As you move tasks, the app indicates the tasks being moved and how many times they've been moved. It also color codes your tasks so you can't overlook them. When it's time to do a task, it sends reminders through your Gmail, Twitter, also as an instant message. You can do this on your smartphone or PC. It's a great way of keeping track of your day-to-day activities to improve organization and productivity.

- **Asana:** The Asana app is a useful tool for breaking down large projects into smaller chunks. You can make a to-do list and break it down into sub-checklists. You can set dates for each task, chat with team members, send and receive files and images, and view upcoming tasks. For ADHD adults, they no longer feel overwhelmed by large tasks and find it easy to transition from one to another as they can see upcoming tasks before it's time for them.

There are several other helpful apps that people with ADHD can use in setting up a home schedule, school, schedule, work schedule and so on. It keeps them in check and organized.

The Role of Visual Aids: Timers and Calendars

Some kids don't like going to school, some will prefer to sleep late into the morning, while others would rather play the whole day till they sleep off wherever the play ends. If you leave your child alone, before you return, the state of your house will tell the story of your absence. That's why it's important you create a structure for your kids.

Your kids depend on you to tell them what to do when they're young, and to guide them as they grow older. Kids with ADHD depend on you for an even longer time. They have special needs, so, you need to do all you can to ensure their life flows in the right direction. One way to do this is through visual aids.

It's said that kids remember what they see more than what they hear. Visual aids like a visual calendar and a visual timer can keep kids on track all day.

Time Management and Organization

A visual calendar consists of a daily schedule written in a simplified form with the right illustrations (pictures) attached.

A visual calendar indicates the activities to do in the morning, at noon, and at night. So, you can draw it (DIY), or print out the right images. In the morning, you have to wake up at 7 am with a picture of someone waking up, then lay in your bed, with the time and right image too, and so on.

A visual timer is a timer designed to show how much time is left for an activity. It functions like an hourglass. If you set the timer for one hour, it begins to read, but as time progresses, a color (red, blue, etc.) covers the part of the time that has passed. The areas that are white show you how much time you have left. The color keeps moving with time till it's an hour and it closes up.

Visual aids like these give kids a program to follow. The visuality makes it easy for them to understand what they have to do next. If you tell them what to do, they may forget or for ADHD kids, they may take it as an instruction and keep working up about it because they know it'll be hard to remember. But when they can see what they have to do, it makes it easy for them to understand and do it.

Again, visual aids help kids stay focused and manage their time. Having what to do at every time of the day keeps kids on track and productive. They're able to manage time because they can see their timer running. So, even ADHD kids who easily get distracted will try to stay focused so they can be done with their tasks before the color on their timer closes up. This way, they are managing their time without even knowing. The color on the timer can make time seem like fun for kids because they will feel happy when they finish a task before time just to watch as the color closes up.

Furthermore, visual aids give kids balance in life and make their days fun and something to look forward to. As you structure their calendar by adding different fun activities and playtime at certain times during each day, it makes them eager to see the calendar for the next day. It also keeps them motivated to do other activities so they can get to the time of play. As you mix their activities - reading, school, play, chores, etc. - it gives their life balance. So they're not stuck on books all day or play all day. Every area of their lives is covered. They read, play, rest, and still do house chores.

As you make their visual aids, place them in places that they can easily access. You can have one placed on the fridge, another in their room, and another at the front door. You can even place it on the dining table and in the kitchen. So anywhere they go, they know what they're to do at that time, and what to do next. It makes the transition easy for them.

Decluttering and Organization: A Zen Approach

As a human, so many things will take your time, especially work. This may leave you little or no time to put your house in order every day. You may be out in the morning, and back in the evening. You're all tired and just want to eat and sleep. For ADHD adults, especially those who live alone or even have a room, theirs is worse. Since they can't put things in order naturally, everywhere will be a mess. But they can somehow live comfortably in it.

Cluttering doesn't always start big. It starts small like leaving leftover pizza on the sink or leaving the coffee cup on the table before leaving for work. When you're back, you get something to eat and put everything in the sink. Before the end of the week, your kitchen begins to stink, and your room is a mess from leaving clothes and shoes all around.

But since you can't do without eating with plates or wearing clothes that will get dirty, you need to learn the art of decluttering and organization. Decluttering is removing the clutter or mess you've made. It's high time your room, kitchen, or workspace looked neat and we'll organize.

I need you to know that something can be clean but not organized. So, it's not enough to wash the clothes. After washing and drying, you need to press the ones that need to be pressed and arrange all of them properly in the closet. That's what decluttering and organization is all about.

For ADHD adults, it can be overwhelming to start cleaning your cluttered room or workspace all at a go. So, here are some tips to help you clean up and organize using the Zen Approach.

Number one is to pick up after yourself. It solves the problem in the present. What do I mean? When you eat, wash the plate. When you remove something from its pack, throw the pack in the waste bag. When you come home from work, take your shoes with you to the place it's to be and keep it there. Same thing with your clothes. Ensure it doesn't touch the floor because once that cloth touches the floor, it's like the strength to pick it up dissolves and it begins to look okay on the floor.

Secondly, shelf your work and declutter your table. At the office or your workspace, ensure your table is not filled with too many papers. Always shelf documents. To make it easy to find, adopt library techniques. Divide your shelf into sections and name each section. Write and paste the name on the section. So once you're done with a file, locate its section and put it there. It'll keep your table clear.

Again, have a container to hold your pen or pencils. You should even have a phone stand if possible so it doesn't get buried in all that paper. At the end of work each day, ensure files, pens and the rest are in their appropriate location before leaving.

Thirdly, choose a free day to declutter, and take it bit by bit. You can start with the room or kitchen. Make a list of what you need to do in the room and then begin. Take it one at a time till you're done. You can then take a break before heading to another part of the house.

Also, when you're decluttering, trash anything that you don't use. Some people like keeping the pack of certain things they've bought and used, while some just forget it in the room. Anything that is not useful to you, remove, and the ones that you can give out, pack them in a box and give them out. Don't just pack it and keep it. You can send it as a donation somewhere.

Again, don't be in a hurry to get new things that you don't need so you don't fill the house up again. Have a day and a particular time that you take out the trash. As you declutter and remove unwanted things, always put the wanted ones in their right places. Let everything be organized.

Takeaway Seven

While organizational skills come easy for some people, kids and adults with ADHD find it difficult to stay organized or even have the motivation to be organized.

Hence, to help them stay on track, this chapter focused on sharing tools: manual, interactional, visual, and technological organizational aids, that can be used in helping them stay organized. These tools will optimize their productivity. Bear in mind that reward is an essential part of employing these tools. The more the reward, the more encouraged ADHD patients will be to stay on track.

Part 3

Nurturing Success in School and Beyond

Kids with ADHD have a hard time with school and social interactions. However, you'll agree with me that these are key areas in their lives that they can't live without. Do you want your ADHD child to have friends their age come around and play with them? Do you also want to see your ADHD child master their condition, and grow into a successful person? Acquiring knowledge and skills to nurture ADHD kids to the point of excellence in school and beyond is inevitable. Good thing is this: that's what you're about to discover in the next few flips.

Chapter 8

Academic Success

Trust yourself; you know more than you think you do.
—**Benjamin Spock**

When parents and teachers collaborate to help kids with special needs, they're laying the bedrock for transforming a difficult situation into a stream of joy. Although that's not always the case, Sarah was fortunate to receive such help. Sarah lives just a few blocks away. She's a problematic ADHD kid with a lot of creative talents. Her talents could easily be dismissed for arrogance and unseriousness. However, her parents tried to see past her tantrums and negative behavioral patterns to concentrate on her talents. That was the turning point for Sarah.

Together with her teachers support, a special, personalized learning plan was designed for her, which entailed chunks of tasks instead of the bulky ones for normal students, and frequent feedback to keep her going.

Sarah got as much as that, and the neighborhood is glad her parents made those choices even when they seemed unpopular. Every child can excel regardless of their peculiarities, they only need peculiar attention.

Homework Challenges: Tips for Productivity

After a long day at school, the kids return with homework and getting them to do it becomes a parent's nightmare. It's hard to get a kid to sit down, and when you do, to get him to concentrate on homework is a big challenge. This challenge gets bigger when you have ADHD kids. It's estimated that parents spend around 6.2 hours per week on homework, while 46.5% of parents find their kids' homework difficult to solve (Drew, 2023).

Naturally, they already find it difficult to sit in class or concentrate. Now they come home and you still want them to do more school work? How do you handle that? How can you make your ADHD child (or neurotypicals) sit, concentrate, and complete their homework on time? There are a few helpful tips that you can adopt to improve your child's academic productivity.

The first is to get them settled and happy after school. When your child returns from school, give them a big hug, ask how their day went, and ensure their meal is ready. You can even list out some fun activities that are on your visual calendar for the day. All of these are to settle their minds and keep them happy. When you ask your child how the day went, their reply will tell you if they're happy or sad. If they're sad, probably because they were bullied due to their condition, you can adopt verbal reinforcement to make them feel better. They need to feel better and happy if you hope to get them to do their homework.

Secondly, institute a fixed time for homework. Always fix homework time two hours after they've returned from school, or in the evening. It shouldn't be immediately after school. These times are best because they are more active and awake than at night. It also gives them time to do other fun things after homework. This fixed schedule is possible if their daily schedule is constant, but if they start having other activities after school hours, you can fix a better time. If you have to move the time for any reason, ensure you inform your child a day before and keep reminding them, especially ADHD kids.

You can also create a serene and distraction-free environment for them to study in, especially ADHD kids. Design a part of the house or their rooms in a way that it's only for studying and doing homework. Remove all forms of distraction like phones, TV, games, teddies, etc. This kind of environment will put them in a studying mood and keep them focused.

To further keep them focused, make the work time-bound. Set a timer and place it before them so they can be conscious of the task at hand. However, a timer may not be enough motivation for an ADHD child to stay focused. So, you need to help them by being a part of their homework hour. Stay with them, answer their questions, and draw their attention to their work when you notice they're lost.

In addition, you can break down their tasks into small parts and in minutes. ADHD kids may get bored if they're doing the same homework for over an hour and it's possible because they find it difficult to concentrate and can spend 3-4 hours on one homework. So, if they have Math and English homework to do, and each has 10 questions, you can break it. They can start with 5 Maths questions (or English if they prefer it to Maths), for 30 minutes to 1 hour. After that, they get a 5-10 minute break. Then return to another 5 questions in the next subject. You can switch subjects till they're done.

One final motivation that can make them stay focused and finish on time is a reward. It can be that you'd let them play a game they like, ask for anything they want, or get screen time. The motivation should be something they value and work to get it. You can even ask what they'll like and use that as the motivation. Never forget, if you make a promise to give them something, ensure you do give it to them. If you don't, you will make them sad and they won't trust you next time.

Effective Parent-Teacher Communication

The educational institution plays a huge role in shaping the lives of kids. That's because they spend almost half their day at school from Monday to Friday for as long as the session lasts. They meet people with different attitudes beliefs, and backgrounds, and these include bullies, social media freaks, cool guys, nerds, weirdos, etc., so there are lots of influences found in an educational environment.

So, school influences a child academically, socially, and morally. Therefore as a parent, you should not ignore the educational life of your child. Don't make the mistakes some parents make by waiting till their kids are back from school to ask how their day went. Don't also wait to be called in by the principal to address your child's misconduct before you get involved.

Get involved in your child's academic life from the first day at school till the last of each grade. One way to know more about your child's school life is through their teachers. Teachers are the ones with the kids at school, teaching, instructing, and correcting them. They are the ones who mark the scripts and know when a kid is improving or not.

Therefore, creating a parent-teacher communication link will do you a whole lot of good. You can ask your kid's teachers to keep you regularly updated on how your kid is faring academically, their fears in class, what they're most corrected on, their behavior, and their overall academic and mental welfare.

If your child returns with a not-so-good report card, you can communicate with the teacher of each subject and ask why your child didn't do well and what areas he needs to work on. Teachers can also send homework and reports to parents to keep them informed on their child's progress. This way, you will know where and how to help your child academically.

Here are some communication avenues for parent-teacher communication.

- You can meet with your child's teacher when you drop him off at school or when you pick them up after school. This is for busy parents who can't make out a lot of time to come see the teachers. You can just spend a few minutes asking questions on how your child is faring at school.

- Another means is through emails, phone calls, social media platforms, and even good old letters or report cards. You can call or chat with your child's teachers from time to time.

- Another place you can meet is at Parent-Teacher conferences/meetings. Here, the progress or failure levels of students is discussed and ways to aid their success are proposed.

- One-on-one with teachers. You can take time from your busy schedule to pay your child's teachers a visit at school during break periods or after school hours. You can agree with the teacher on the time and get all the details you want. Also, ask how you can be of help to your kid's academic performance.

Communicating regularly with your kid's teachers gives you an understanding of how your child spends almost half of this day. You get to understand their struggles and strengths. Your child will also feel loved and valued, which will make it easier for them to tell you about their emotional and otherwise struggles at school.

Mindful Learning Strategies: Study Techniques

When it comes to academics, a lot of students today—some pressured by their parents— focus more on writing exams and getting good grades they can show off or that their parents can be proud of. While preparing for exams, they engage in memorization and flippant studying. Most of these students cannot remember what they read a few days after writing the exam. Once they're done with one subject, they move to the next. Such contexts of learning won't do an ADHD kid any good. It'll only make them worse. Therefore, a more mindful approach must be designed for their personalized learning.

Some intelligent kids adopt the reading, jotting, memorisation, and asking and answering possible questions methods. This is a good reading strategy but it's not always effective. However, the solution to these issues is mindful learning strategies. Mindful learning strategies are conscious learning strategies that keep your mind full of whatever you're learning. It enables you to be in the present as you learn for better understanding and retention.

The reason this approach is more effective than normal reading habits is because it keeps the mind free and filled with what one is studying. Oftentimes when you read, your mind is full of other things like the activity coming up later, someone you like, or something you have to do later on.

Academic Success

Your mind isn't settled. It takes in information but finds it difficult to file them because there are so many interferences. So you read 10 pages of a subject but at the end, you can only remember a few things.

In mindful learning, all those distractions and interferences in the mind are cleared. It's like writing on a new page. Whatever you write will be clear enough to be read. There are some mindful study techniques that work for both students and employees.

One mindful learning strategy is practicing mindfulness. Just as you've learned in some previous parts of this book, mindfulness exercises focus your mind on the present, and clear out the junk in your mind without you judging yourself for not thinking about them. You can practice mindfulness meditation or breathing, whichever your time can take. Do this whenever you want to read or your mind begins to wander in class. Mindfulness breathing always comes in handy.

Another strategy is metacognition. This simply means thinking about what you're thinking. You may be reading and think you're focused on what you're reading, but the truth is that if you think about it, there are other thoughts running in the background of your mind. It's estimated that 46.9% of the day, people's thoughts wander from what they're doing (Bradt, 2019). That means the probability of you studying while your mind is playing basketball somewhere else is high.

For some others, they have negative thoughts about subjects. Some kids find math challenging and when it's time to study it, their minds are closed to it. They just do it because it's necessary. Try to encourage such kids to conduct a self-assessment, you'll discover that their understanding of the subject they dread is tied to their perception of that subject. In that case, they'll find it hard to understand even the simplest equation because they've already programmed their mind to believe it's difficult.

During the self-assessment, encourage them to ask themselves how much they understand after studying, why they don't understand 90% of what they study, how effective their study method is, and what is their perception about each subject and even the teachers who teach them. You see, if you dislike your English teacher, you will not find English easy. The state of your mind plays a huge role in how much you learn, understand, and retain information.

One way they can overcome these negative thoughts is by believing in neuroplasticity. This is another effective strategy, but it's more of a change in your brain than a physical study method. Neuroplasticity is the creation of new pathways in your brain, or simply put, it's the new connection of neurons in your brain. What does this mean?

Neurons are messenger cells in your brain and they are in billions. They transfer a particular information by connecting till you get the message. It's these neurons that make it easy for you to reprogram your mind or learn something new. When you begin to learn something new or change a negative thought line to a positive one, a new connection of neurons begins to transmit information about that new activity. The more you carry out that activity, the stronger the connection gets.

With this knowledge, you can help an ADHD kid change their negative thoughts and study habits, and help them learn a mindful study strategy. As they practice mindful learning, you'll notice over time that their concentration, understanding, and retention levels during studying will increase.

Nurturing a Growth Mindset in Your Child

Parents need to instil growth mindset in their kids, and not just focus all their energies on nourishing them with meals for physical growth. Some kids have fixed mindsets, which means they don't think they can do better than they are already doing. They just feel satisfied with their level of development and avoid any task that will take them out of that comfort zone. But a growth mindset means believing there's always room for improvement.

It's knowing that you can be and do better. You fix your interest in what you're learning, not even on what you're to gain from it like good grades. It's a mindset that keeps you learning and discovering new things and new ways of doing old ones. Some kids with ADHD kids may find it difficult to adopt this mindset because the evidence caused by their condition says otherwise.

So you need to teach your kids to disabuse their minds from a fixed mindset, and encourage them to adopt a growth mindset.

You can do this by telling them stories and "showing" them. It's easy to do something if someone else has done it before. Tell your kids stories (realistic or forged) of kids or adults who are successful even with ADHD. They can also learn from watching movies about people with a growth mindset and how well they did. It can be cartoons or educational videos.

Secondly, you want to keep encouraging them. Be their personal cheerleader. Recite a positive mantra with them every morning before they leave the house. When they fail in a task, show them how well they've done by even attempting it. Teach them the importance of failure to become successful. If they have a positive understanding of failure, they will not be afraid of failing.

Failure is just a way to know it's not the right way of doing something. It means, " Try something else". So, failure is progress. Plus, failing doesn't mean they're a failure. You can tell them stories of when you failed and how you bounced back so they will know failure is common and not particular to them.

Again, guide them in their tasks and when they get it right, reward them and reinforce the positivity and growth mindset. You can also introduce a new task each week. It'll help them learn new things. These new tasks can be games or fun exercises, but let it be different every week or month. Encourage them to learn new things, meet new people, take them to museums, art galleries, and parks, and let them see new things. It'll open up their minds to see the world of possibilities.

Lastly, be their role model. Practice learning new things from time to time and let them know. You can even get them involved. For example, you can choose to learn how to make a dish you've never made before, then you can get them involved. If you guys fail at it, laugh over it and try again some other day. When they see that you don't give up even after failing, they'll learn not to.

Addressing Bullying and Peer Interactions

Bullying is a term that is associated with hurt and pain but has somehow become common in schools today. Statistics show that 10% of kids drop out of school due to bullying (Loveless, 2010). When you think of bullying, physical harm may come to mind, but there are other forms of bullying.

There is verbal bullying where kids say hurtful words to their peers and use their weakness against others as a point of mockery. There's also social bullying where a student spreads a rumor about another student or leaks their secret online.

The truth is that bullying of any kind has negative effects on the bullied and these effects can last till they become adults. They may spend their lives running away from doing that one thing they're criticized about, or spend their lives doing it just to prove they are good. Still, they won't feel any satisfaction from doing it and the taunts will just keep hunting their minds.

The bullies in school are often kids from wealthy homes or big and bitter kids. They bully kids who aren't outspoken or have a defect, like ADHD kids. Parents and teachers therefore need to find ways to address this issue in order to reduce the rate of bullying at schools.

One method they can adopt is enlightenment. It's important teachers enlighten their students on the negative effects of bullying both on the bullied and also on the bullied. The bully is never truly happy because they bully out of bitterness or negligence of some kind and just pour it out through bullying. Tell them the benefits of helpful peer interactions and why it's important for them to watch each other's back.

Secondly, make rules that are against bullying. Let there be a punishment for bullies. Let the school create a clandestine and confidential avenue where those who are bullied can make a report. As a teacher or a parent, you also need to be sensitive to your student's/child's behavior. Be watchful if you'll notice any change in their behavior, or if they suddenly don't want to go to school again, or come home hiding their hands or holding somewhere in pain, or a brilliant student suddenly becomes quiet and dull in class

When you notice any of these, don't overlook it or give excuses for it. Don't also postpone asking them. Bullied kids are always scared and feel insecure, so it's not easy for them to open up. It's best if you plan a day to talk to them. On that day, take them to a quiet place or let them do something they like. After a while, you can tell them a story of someone who was bullied. You can then slowly move into asking them if they're being bullied at school or elsewhere.

Know that bullying doesn't just occur in school. It can occur at home or on the street. Once you identify the place where this bullying happens, especially if it's in school, report it to the appropriate authorities. You also need to help that child heal. Try to make them happy, remove the threat, and emphasize how brilliant they are to build their self-confidence.

Parents who have bullies as children, shouldn't cover up for them. Listen to why they've chosen that path and teach them, love them, and watch them. If you don't train your child right now, they may grow to be your worst nightmare.

Kids should be taught to love their peers and say kind words to those struggling with one challenge or another. They should be taught empathy, kindness, and being helpful. They should also be taught to stand up for anyone they see being bullied and report the bully to the right authority.

School Accommodations and IEPs: Navigating the System

Kids with disorders like ADHD always find learning a bit more difficult than their counterparts. That's why there are some special schools for some of them. However, as important as a special school is, it somehow makes their life difficult when they're done and have to face the world.

This is why The Individualized Educational Plan (IEP) permits the enrollment of kids with disabilities into regular elementary and secondary schools (public or private) (Cassata, 2022).

When they associate with normal kids, they'll learn how the world works. They'll learn the challenges they have to face, ensure, and overcome to be relevant in normal society.

But inasmuch as they're allowed to join normal (or neurotypical) kids, they don't automatically become normal. Their learning challenges are still there. They'll still find it difficult to concentrate, stay in a place, remember certain instructions, or complete projects and homework on time.

That's why IEP therefore has a law that states that normal schools that enroll kids with special needs have to provide appropriate adaptable study techniques and special educational services for them. It means that there should be suitable accommodation, adaptation, and modifications to meet the educational needs of these kids.

An IEP team consists of the parents of the disabled, their teachers, and some other service providers. They come together to evaluate the child's performance, skill set, possible modifications, goals, and the end result they hope to see.

The modification, adaptation, and accommodation the school provides make their learning easy. An example of modification is making their tasks and assignments simpler. If other kids have 10 questions, an ADHD child should have 5. Then, accommodation is a change in the learning system to accommodate or make the work they do easier. For example, while other kids have an hour to finish their exam, ADHD kids should be given 2 hours. They should also be kept in a seat in front of the teacher, away from distraction.

Adaption on the other hand is a change in the materials of these kids. They would still learn the same thing but in a way, they can adapt to it. So, if they can't concentrate enough to write out an answer, they can say it. While other kids copy their homework, ADHD kids can have a visual aid to help them understand the homework, and the teacher can break it into sections.

These are all ways schools can make learning easy for disabled kids. Teachers will be patient enough with them, and not push them like they would other kids. They should consider them when setting a pop quiz. They should write more than they dictate, and use pictures and videos to teach if possible. They can intertwine their classes with interesting stories that will keep ADHD kids concentrated and make them gain interest in the subject.

Now, teachers may not be able to control how other students see these special needs kids or what they say to them, but it also helps them to gain resilience and determination. No matter how much taunting they get, they'll still make some neurotypical friends too and this will help them know how to interact socially when they go out into the world.

Preparing for Transitions: Grade Changes and New School

Transition is a common happening in life. It begins from the womb when a fetus becomes a baby, then a walking child, to an adolescent and then to an adult. As common as transitions are, it's never easy to transition from one phase to another, but when you successfully do, after a while, you get used to it.

It's the same with kids who move from one grade to another, or have to change their school because the family relocated or for some other reason. It can be hard on them as they are filled with anxiety about the people they'll meet, the curriculum and the teachers they'll meet in the new school. It's like moving from the known to the unknown.

It's almost harder for those who had to relocate because then, it's not only the new school the kids have to adapt to, but also the new street, house, neighbors, and environment. They'll also miss their friends, favorite stores, favorite teachers, an activity in school that they really like, and all they are used to.

Parenting ADHD with Empathy And Effectiveness

For those kids transitioning from one grade to another, they get anxious about meeting new teachers, new and higher academic demands, and all the pressure that comes with something new. Nevertheless, you have a part to play in helping your kid (either changing grades or school) prepare for and fit into their new level/school.

The first thing you should do is have a tête-à-tête (intimate) conversation with them. You can take them somewhere private or a restaurant and talk about their fears and anxiety. Make them feel comfortable to share their feelings, and then listen to them actively. At that moment, you're not to give advice or scold or belittle their feelings. Instead, validate their feelings. You can even share your transition experience while growing up.

When you're done, comfort them. Use positive words to make them know everything will be fine. Let them know that you care and that you're there for them. Then, you can start talking about the good things they stand to gain in their new grade or school. Paint a mental picture for them about the facilities of the new school, how interesting it will be, or the privileges and growth that come with a new grade.

To further facilitate your point, bring the image to life by taking them on a tour of the school before they officially resume. If there are activities in this school that they were interested in which was also in their former school, that's a good place to start. Show them other exciting areas and things they can learn in the new school that their old school didn't have.

This way, their thoughts will no longer be, "This is really bad". It'll begin to soften to be, "This can be interesting". They'll begin to imagine and see possibilities in this transition. To further get them elated, take them shopping for their new uniforms, books, and other academic materials they'd be needing. Also, tell them how far you've gone in their registration and when they're to resume. This will prepare their mind.

In order to make them feel better, you can find a way to reach their closest old friends. It can be through phone calls (if you relocated), Skype, or a night out for them (if you're still in the same environment), or you can invite them for lunch via their parents.

All of these steps will prepare your child's mind and give them a smooth transition from one level to another.

Takeaway Eight

Some kids find academic work tasking, especially ADHD kids, so you need to make it interesting and encourage them as necessary as possible. This chapter consists of recommendations on how to achieve this with an ADHD kid. Through mindful learning strategies and active involvement in their school life place them on a pedestal of academic success. With the implementation of policies like IEP, too, an ADHD kid stands the chance of excelling academically.

Chapter 9

Building Positive Relationships

"It is not our purpose to become each other; it is to recognize each other, to learn to see the other and honor him for what he is."
—Hermann Hesse

Social Challenges in ADHD: Isolation and Rejection

In a grade 1 class, everyone hated Peter. He always received special attention from the teacher and even when he made a mistake, the teacher would smile at him and correct him, but it's different for the other kids.

After classes, Peter is so active and wanted to talk but no one wants to talk to him. One day, he saw a group of his classmates discussing and joined them. Immediately, he started talking because he couldn't wait his turn. While he was still, Lizzy said to him, "Peter, you talk too much", and everyone walked away.

Peter felt so rejected. He knew something was wrong with him, he didn't behave like others, but he couldn't help it. From then on, he decided to hide in his shell and never come out again.

Peter's story is a glimpse into the lives of ADHD kids. Their symptoms make social interaction difficult for them. They know they're different, but they can't help how they act and react and these are the core of social relationships.

Naturally, kids are innocent and open and easily make friends, but they cringe and go away if they find their friend repulsive. They're unlike adults who have the capacity to want to try and understand why the person acts that way and how to adapt. Their emotional intelligence is still developing so it's hard for them to keep friends who act "weird".

This is why ADHD kids have it hard when it comes to making or keeping friends. First of all, they are hyperactive. They find it difficult to stay at a place in class like other kids, and that alone is weird. Aside from that, they are always talking about multiple subjects and won't let anyone else into the conversation.

Even when they talk to others, their friends can't understand what they are talking about. Even when they understand, before they can make a contribution, the topic may have changed to something else. Again, when ADHD kids are talking with others in a group, they can just butt in while someone is still talking.

This kind of attitude can make the other children feel stupid and less appreciated, and it looks like they are less intelligent. This will further drive them away from their ADHD peers.

Some ADHD kids are inattentive. After saying what is in their minds, they can't listen to another person talk. They get distracted in the middle of a conversation and look uninterested in what others are saying or doing as long as they don't like it. They go on to do what they like without considering if anyone else likes it.

Furthermore, they are impulsive and cannot control their emotions. They may be playing with some kids now, and later start shouting or beating other kids because they didn't like something that happened or the game isn't going the way they want. They react instantly and forcefully to whatever disturbs them emotionally. They can even harm themselves or others. They can make drastic decisions like tearing their books or running away. They can even say hurtful things without thinking about how the other person feels.

All these plus the fact that they get to have special attention from the teachers make other kids stay away from them. These ADHD kids will therefore be rejected so many times by other kids. Let's say the teacher wants to pair kids to carry out project work, no one will like to be paired with him.

Or, a student may be inviting everyone for their birthday party, but wouldn't invite him. Sometimes, he may be walking and other kids will start whispering about his behavior. During breaks, no one wants to play or eat with him. That makes him feel rejected.

The fact that they can't control what is happening to them is another challenge. After a period of social trial and error, they would switch to isolation mode. They feel hurt that no one wants to talk to them, and they don't want to hurt others, so they begin to withdraw from everyone. They become more self-conscious in trying to reduce their symptoms.

All of these can lead to increased anxiety, frustration, and depression. It will then affect their academic performance, their mood, and even affect them in future because you see, everyone needs a friend.

Teaching Compassion and Empathy

Humans are naturally born with the traits of sympathy and empathy. You will notice it in a baby who smiles at his mother's facial expression or stops crying in appreciation or response to his father trying to make him happy. You can see it in how your kid goes to comfort his crying sister whose toy was taken away from her.

So kids have the ability to be both empathetic and sympathetic. However, these attributes aren't already made. They are like planted seeds. For them to grow, you need to water them and tend them. Kids only act that way due to the mirror neurons in their brains that mirror the feelings of others to them (Pera, 2023).

That's why you see that this brother that is consoling his sister now, can see his friend angry and all he's thinking about is how to play. When the friend refuses to play, he gets angry and leaves without considering that his friend is angry.

Nevertheless, empathy and compassion are virtues that every kid should learn, ADHD or not because it shows our humaneness. While empathy refers to being one with the feelings of others, compassion (which can also be called sympathy), means feeling sorry for others and taking action to help solve their problem.

While empathy deals with you sharing someone's emotions—being angry about what makes them angry and being happy about what makes them happy—compassion is a conscious but genuine effort to help someone who is in need without really attaching intense feelings to it. They look like they're the same thing but they're not.

This is what kids need to learn and if you want your child to grow to be kind and caring and loving, you need to start inculcating this attitude in them from their tender age. You can start by teaching them about compassion and empathy, both for themselves, their family members, and others. You see, it seems easier to show outsiders compassion than family members like siblings and parents because of over-familiarity.

So, this charity must begin at home. You should also be a model of these behaviors. Children, especially when they're still very tender, learn a lot from their parents. They learn more from what they see you do than what you say. They watch how to talk to your spouse, and how you react when they or their siblings make a mistake. They watch how you treat neighbors and what you say about them inside the house. They copy your actions, so be a role model for good.

Again, you can role play for them so they can know what a person who isn't happy looks like. You can also use facial expressions, or movies (kids movies of course). As they watch the movie, pause it from time to time when you see someone's expression and ask them what the person is feeling. Then ask how they should react when they see someone like that.

When they watch and hear about compassion and empathy time and again, they would find it easy to identify and show these virtues to someone who needs them. You need to be watchful of this. When you see your ADHD kid saying sorry to her sibling she yelled at, or when you see one of your kids trying to help a neighbor's kid, be sure to praise that child.

You can even give him a token as encouragement. You may not see them do it, but if your kid runs to you to narrate how he helped or comforted someone, listen too with the same excitement even if you're not "in the mood" and commend them for their efforts. The more you do this, the deeper the lesson will run in them.

Mindful Social Skills: Communication and Conflict Resolution

A man vowed not to quarrel with anyone, but he knew living with people would lead to a quarrel one day. So, one fine morning, he got up, packed his bag and headed for the mountains. He saw a cave there and decided to live there, away from humans so he would never have problems with anyone.

After two weeks, he ran out of supplies and had to come to town to get some. He went to a store, took what he needed, paid for it, and left. He continued to do this for over a month. One day, he went to get supplies at the store as usual, and as usual, he went to pay for it. But at the counter, he discovered a new attendant. He was a young man, probably in his early twenties, with a body full of tattoos and a pierced nose.

The man couldn't take his eyes off the young man. In his mind, he was wondering how painful it must have been to take all that tattoo. His eyes were just fixed on the young man.

After checking his stuff, the young man looked up only to see the man staring at him. He then got offended because of the man's facial expression, saying that the man was giving him a dirty look, and a quarrel erupted.

It's almost impossible to go through life without conflicts. That's because people have different emotional responses, and see things differently. As long as you live with and around people, conflict will always arise

Building Positive Relationships

Conflict is a strong disagreement between two people or more people on a matter that seems important to them. Due to the presence of conflict, it's important to develop the skill of mindful conflict resolution because it's key in establishing and growing social relations. One factor that can help you do this is mindful communication.

Mindful communication is the ability to express yourself precisely and firmly while choosing your words carefully in a way that won't hurt others. Mindful conflict resolution, on the other hand, is applying strategies to settle a conflict between two or more people amicably to foster forgiveness and peace.

Mindful communication means you have to consider how others will feel before you say something, even when you're hurt. You shouldn't pour out your emotions the way it is even if your words hurt others. You need to learn to be mindful, that is, present as you communicate with others. This is a skill you also need to teach your kids.

When you learn to communicate mindfully, it makes the other person patient enough to listen to you and strengthens relationships. The person sees you as mature and you gain their confidence. Mindful speaking doesn't mean saying things to please the other person while displeasing yourself. It means stating your feelings about something clearly and emphatically while using kind words.

When your kids learn this, they will know how to talk to their peers, and even teachers without starting a conflict. Nevertheless, conflict cannot be completely avoided. Once in a while, your opinion may disagree with that of another. In this case, practice mindful conflict resolution. In practicing mindful conflict resolution, you don't want to ignore how you feel or accept you're wrong just to keep the peace. That's not the aim. That doesn't help, it only makes things bad for you.

In practicing mindful conflict resolution, calmly share your feelings about the reaction of the other person to what you said and how it hurt you. Then, listen and try to understand -not judge- the other person's perspective and why they did what they did. When you listen with an open mind like this, you'll see where you went wrong and acknowledge it.

As you speak, you're not defining the person's character by that one behavior. You're discussing the problem separately from the person and you should always use "I", not "you". When both parties know what they did wrong and what caused the conflict in the first place, the next thing is forgiveness.

Both parties should apologize, forgive themselves, and let go of the grudge. But now, they both know how to react in that kind of situation if it arises again. In mindful conflict resolution, the aim is not to go separate ways, but to forgive one another and form a stronger bond.

Practicing mindful communication and conflict resolution helps you establish your relationships. I mean, you can't keep cutting off from anyone who offends you. You will end up alone because even your kids will offend you. So, these soft skills are effective social bonding tools everyone, kids and adults alike, must learn.

Group Activities for Strengthening Friendships

Adults and kids alike (with ADHD or not) all need a friend, but good friends are hard to come by. Good friends are dependable, understanding, compassionate, and trustworthy. When you find such friends, it's important you do all you can to keep and strengthen such friendships. It's not enough to call them to share your sorrow or joy.

There are lots of fun activities for both kids and adults that will aid in creating a stronger bond between themselves and their friends. I'll start with group activities for kids. For one, you should encourage your kids to have good friends. That's the first thing to do. Then again, you need to know their friends. You don't want to be the propeller of a bad friendship.

Kids become friends with whoever Interests them, whether they are good or bad. So you should know the character of your child's friends. Encourage

Building Positive Relationships

your child to let you know when they make a new friend, then ask them to come over for lunch or breakfast on a weekend. You can get permission from their parents. There you can analyze the kid's character.

When you're sure of the friends your kids have, you can then plan a game or movie night/sleepover. This is always a good way for kids to bond. Plan an agenda for their sleepover like saying what you like about yourselves, what you'd like to be in future, likes and dislikes both in character and meals, etc. It should be questions or statements that will make them know each other more.

Another fun activity for kids bonding, at school or at home, is doing a project together. It can be papercraft, painting, or floor puzzles. Whatever the project you chose, it shouldn't be done individually. It should be one project and they all get to contribute their ideas on how to get it done. This is both fun and educational. They will have to put ideas together, work as a team, and see the importance of everyone on the team due to their contribution.

Friendship is all about being there for each other and sharing in your pains and joys. You can teach them to connect with each other emotionally through role play, music, dance, and play. Teach them to come up with stories, just give them a theme, and let them act it out. Again, let them play together and if anyone falls or gets injured, others should find ways to help. Dancing is also another fun activity that binds people. The more they see each other, the closer they'll get.

For adults on the other hand, you can plan a spa day, go to the beach, go for a picnic, visit the cinema house, plan a vacation, have a sleepover, go camping, etc. I know adults don't easily open up like kids do, but that's why you want to create a bond. Friendship isn't about laughing and playing and gossiping. It's more than that.

These activities should be conscious and intimate moments where you all share your feelings. It should be a time of bonding physically and emotionally. You can even have a secret handshake and nicknames for yourselves. I know things like work, family, finance, and so on may not let you guys meet often, so, ensure you're always in touch.

Make conference calls or conference Skype. The more you keep in touch, the easier it will be for anyone going through a challenge can open up about it because love and care exist in the group. You may end up being closer to one or two persons in the group, and that's okay. Just ensure your connection is strong as a group.

Building Healthy Boundaries: Friendship Dos and Don'ts

Whenever David sees Kelvin coming over to play with him, he suddenly feels uncomfortable. It's not because he doesn't like playing with Kelvin, but Kelvin likes taunting his younger sister, Malvis because she has ADHD.

Kelvin says Malvis doesn't act like a "proper" girl because she's always "all over the place", and talks too much. Kelvin would shout at her whenever she came to talk to David, interrupting their play without as much as an, "Excuse me". She just butts in and talks unendingly. When Kelvin shouts at her, she runs into her room and cries. This always hurts David.

One day, David couldn't take it anymore. He liked to play with Kelvin and he didn't want to lose their friendship but he also wanted to protect his sister. So one day, when Kelvin came around to play, David moved their play place from the front of the house where his sister liked playing, to the back of the house. He then calmly explained to Kelvin why his sister acts that way and asked that Kelvin never insulted his sister again.

As much as you value the sincere opinions of your friends and the fact that they can say them, there have to be boundaries. Your friends are still humans, and humans sometimes do or say things you consider offensive. You must be the one to establish this boundary and this goes for both adults and kids.

A boundary is like a line your friends can't cross. It's a borderline you set - emotional, physical, intellectual - that your friends aren't allowed to cross. Setting healthy boundaries strengthens friendship and creates a sense of order and respect for each other.

Building Positive Relationships

These boundaries can be the principles you uphold that mustn't be tampered with, or your likes and dislikes. You can set these boundaries at the beginning of a friendship or somewhere in the middle. In setting healthy boundaries, you need to apply mindful communication. You want to be assertive about what you expect and what you can't tolerate, but you also don't want to come off as bossy or arrogant (Pattemore, 2021).

If you're not sure what boundaries you should set, here are some tips to help you find out.

- Are you uncomfortable around a particular friend?
- What do they do that puts you off inside but you just don't say it?
- How do you want to be treated?
- What do you expect from your friends?

When you're able to answer these questions, you will find the answers you seek. You see, some people act and react based on the influence of their temperament. While some people can be so forward and outgoing, some others are conservative and indifferent.

You may be the quiet type but have a "loud" friend. You may like it when she pushes you to go out more and how she helps you make new friends, but you may not like the way she easily gives out your information to a stranger. You may not also like how she butts into a conversation you're having with a family member or a spouse.

This is a boundary you have to set, otherwise, the friendship may grow sour one day. In setting this boundary, you need to call her and mildly but assertively tell her what you don't like and what you expect from her. This way, everyone is on the same page.

In setting boundaries, you must be true to how you feel and communicate it in the mildest way possible. If there's a topic you and your friends disagree on (be it religion, beliefs, family history, etc.), set a boundary not to discuss that topic. If you're the type that gets edgy when you're emotionally unstable, tell them so that when you're in that mood, they won't come around until you're calm.

If you're married and you're not okay with how your friends behave when they come over to the house, then tell them, or move your meetings to a restaurant or somewhere else. If you're not okay with it when someone calls on you early in the morning or very late at night, state it. If you're not the party type, state it.

Your boundaries help you not to go against yourself just to please your friends. Your friends should understand and respect it. If they don't, then weigh that friendship. If it's important, you can keep it at arm's length. If it's not, you can walk away from it. Your mental health and wellness is most important.

Setting boundaries doesn't mean you can't make sacrifices for your friends. Of course, you can, but that should be a willing personal decision. For instance, if you're emotionally down, and a friend calls to inform you that she just got "served", or she lost someone, you can prioritize her pain over your discomfort. You can put your pain aside and comfort her. You guys can even go on to share your pains and empathize with one another.

When you know this, also teach your kids to do the same. At school, they should let their friends know that they can't leave the class or skip school to do something else. If you have laid out rules in your family, they should make it clear to any of their friends who come to visit. It's a good and healthy way to build a relationship.

Building Self-Esteem and Resilience in Kids

Self-esteem is an important virtue every child should have if they hope to become successful in life. Yet, this is one virtue that seems far from ADHD kids. Self-esteem, simply put, is knowing your worth. It's the way you see yourself. Some people see themselves as worthless, small, and insignificant. That's what is called low self-esteem.

Building Positive Relationships

As you strive to build healthy self-esteem in your child, you also want to build the spirit of resilience. Resilience is what helps them bounce back from difficult situations and keep moving forward. So, while self-esteem establishes their worth and self-respect, resilience keeps them going irrespective of what they face on their journey to becoming successful individuals.

You can build these virtues in your kids by first, being their cheerleader. If you have an ADHD child, know that they need a daily dose of positive reinforcement. Every day, praise your kids on areas they're good in and show them the beauty in themselves. What they hear from someone dear to them like you, will go a long way in building their self-worth.

Whenever they fail or make a terrible mistake that affects them emotionally, validate their feelings, and help them come out of it. Teach them to stand up for themselves and value themselves by focusing more on their strengths while working on their weaknesses.

Teach them to set personal academic, friendship, and otherwise goals and monitor their progress level. When they complete a goal, give them a reward. As a parent, never overlook your child's feelings. Make them feel valued and important because what your words can't achieve in them, your actions will.

Also, be their role model. Let them learn from you, and you can also share your stories with them, about how you failed at work but bounced back and did better. Teach them to learn to identify and correct their mistakes instead of letting them eat them up.

Again, teach them to look ahead of failures and see the success that follows. Also, teach them self-compassion. Let them have breaks from time to time to shake off pressure and stress. You can take them out for ice cream or a picnic. Encourage them to do what they love when they're feeling overwhelmed and not sulk about it. They should also learn to share their feelings and seek advice.

Without the right self-esteem and resilience, kids can grow to be and achieve less than they should have because they'll find it easy to settle for less. If you want to know if your kid has low self-esteem or not, you can ask them some simple questions like:

- What can you do?

- Do you think you're better than your classmates?

- Are you proud of yourself?

- How do you see yourself?

Now, self-esteem is self-worth or respect. It's different from pride. Pride is thinking you're better than others just to feel good about yourself. If your kid has pride, they'd want to talk others down. That's not it. Self-esteem is knowing, acknowledging, and accepting your strengths and weaknesses. So, if Debbie is good at English, she can say she is good at English even if her friends are not. It's not pride because she's not trying to prove anything to anyone. It's just a fact.

Helping Kids Find Their Passions and Interests

Passion is an inner drive that keeps you on a path. While interest is something you feel drawn to. Their meanings seem to be similar, but there's a little difference. You can have passion for an interest. So passion is the strong feeling you have about something, while interest is something you like doing.

These are key components every kid must possess, and as a parent, you're to help them. Kids need to discover their areas of interests and hobbies, and which they have passion for. A child may love to join her mom in cooking, but will choose a science experiment over cooking any day.

Your boy may love playing football with his friends, but would rather watch his dad fix the car. It means, a child may have many interests, but have a stronger passion for just one or two of such interests. You can help them discover their interests through various means.

Building Positive Relationships

You can start by watching and talking to them. What toys do they play with the most? What always draws their attention? What do they seem overly excited about doing? What do they like to do from time to time? Watching their actions and reactions can tell you what their interests are and which they have the most passion for. You can also talk to them, especially those who are of age. Ask them what they like and why. Make comparisons with what they've told you they like and ask which they'd pick.

Another thing you can do is to give them options. Make different games, sports, play, and activities available to them and let them explore. This will be very helpful for ADHD kids. When they experiment with different options, they will know which they like more, which they like less, and which they'd rather sleep than do it.

Again, give them space to choose. Let them have the autonomy to choose whatever they like. Don't try to change their interests or force one on them because you like it. They may do it just to obey you, but you're taking their personality away from them. Let them make their choices and you should both respect and support their choices. Your work is to journal their interests over time because they will keep changing till they find one.

However, no matter how it changes, it will still run around a circumference. For example, your little girl spends all her free time with her dolls. She feeds them, clothes them, talks to them, and lays them to sleep. Aside from that, whenever she sees any of her siblings sad, she goes and comforts them. She shares her snacks and laughs a lot. As she grows, she may not continue to play with toys but you still notice how she "unconsciously" rushes to someone's aid. These are all signs that she may end up in the medical field.

With this example, you can see that interest isn't limited to what they do alone, but also how they act and react to situations. You need to take note of all these. When you've noticed their area of interest and passion, you should provide all they need to encourage it. If your boy loves basketball, you can get him a shirt from one of his favorite basketball players.

Discovering their interests and passions while they're young can give you a picture of who they may likely choose to be when they grow older. It also prepares your mind as a parent for what is to come (Buchtel, 2022).

Celebrating Progress: Recognizing and Valuing Achievements

Have you ever felt happy about the way a project you're working on is going? Or how well your plans are coming together? Or are you always on your toes until you achieve a goal and then move on to the next?

Some people fail to realize that the process of achieving something is equally as important as the result. You should learn to celebrate the process as we aspire to achieve great things. When you see your ADHD child sitting and reading for 30 minutes or 1 hour without walking about, applaud it. It's true he hasn't gotten an "A" in the exam yet, but you should applaud his effort.

You may not have completed that project but you're making headway. Applaud yourself and set a reward for yourself when you finally complete the project. Learn to see how well you and others around you are doing. Acknowledge and praise the good effort to make something work, and even if it doesn't, don't think your efforts were in vain. It's better to try than to not try. When you try, you know what is possible and what is not.

You should also teach your kids this trait that is quickly diminishing in this fast-paced world. They should appreciate the process. When your ADHD child attempts to make a friend, they should see how they're learning and growing whether it works out or not. Many times we're waiting to hit our target before we celebrate, but that just keeps our anxiety level up and it's like we're holding our breath.

Learn to celebrate both the process and the result. Celebrate when you make a big win personally, as a team, or as a family. Also, celebrate when you make a big win. They're all important. When you celebrate your achievement, it means you value yourself and what you've done.

You shouldn't live a life that revolves around moving from one task to another. You'll get exhausted and you'll be missing out on hold days. When you have a win, hang out with your friends or family and celebrate it. You can take yourself out for a treat and get that cheesecake you always wanted.

When the excitement dies down, take time to think about all you've accomplished. Let the process - the failures you battled with, the sorrowful times, the good times - flow through your mind. Reflect on what you could do better next time to avoid some pitfalls and facilitate success. Learn from every small or big win, and use it to win more.

One thing you should know is that if anyone deserves to win, it's definitely you. Your kids also deserve to win, ADHD or not. As you keep encouraging them and being there for them, their seeming weaknesses will be their greatest strength and you get to take the credit for that.

How delightful that would be! How delightful it'll be to see your ADHD child taking the valedictory speech! How delightful it'd be to see your kids grow to become world changers in their various fields! It all starts from now. Teach them and join them to celebrate their small wins today, and it'll get bigger tomorrow.

Takeaway Nine

We are different but many in this world because we weren't meant to be alone. Everyone needs a friend, kids and adults alike, and when you finally find these friends—the good ones—do all you can to keep them and strengthen your friendship bond.

ADHD kids will benefit more from having a social network they can connect with. Helping them nurture the necessary social skills will make them feel accepted and loved. Hence, enhancing their chances of excelling in different spheres of life. That is the crux of our robust discussion in this book.

Conclusion

Michael Phelps is unarguably the most successful and decorated swimmer of our time. And yes, he has ADHD. He started swimming at the age of 7 and was determined to become one of the greatest swimmers ever. However, while in sixth grade at age 9, he was diagnosed with ADHD, but that didn't stop him. At age 10, he held a national record for the 100-meter butterfly for his age group and didn't stop winning till he retired in 2016.

Michael Fred Phelps II was born on the 30th of June 1985 in Baltimore, Maryland. He was the last of three children. He developed a passion for swimming at age 7, and as his career began to take off, he got a coach, Bob Bowman at age 11. He won lots of swimming competitions and had about 28 medals to his name before he retired.

He attributed his success to his sisters and his ADHD. He got support from his sisters while his ADHD gave him the hyperfocus to chase his dreams. Swimming was also a way of releasing the pent-up energy and restlessness in him due to his disorder. He was resilient, focused on his goal of becoming the greatest Olympian, and he put in the hard work. Phelps was good at his game and so fast, and it earned him the nickname, " Flying Fish".

He said his swimming career began when his mom put him and his sisters in the pool so they could learn to swim. Like most kids, he was afraid of water at first, but after a while, he began to enjoy it. That was when he made up his mind that he'd be one of the greatest swimmers ever. His love for swimming triggered his hyperfocus. At a certain time, he practiced every day for five years without missing a day. His motto was, "Dream, plan, reach". He believed that hard work pays, and it did.

Conclusion

Michael Phelps has set 39 world records more than any other swimmer. He has lots of awards and medals to his name. Here are a few:

- 23 most Olympic Gold Medals
- 13 most medals in single games
- Swimming World World Swimmer of the Year Award in 2003, 2004, 2006, 2007, 2008, 2009, 2012, and 2016
- SwimSwam Swammy Award for the make swimmer of the year 2016
- Marca Leyenda Award in 2008
- Sports Illustrated Sportsman of the Year in 2008 and 2012
- 2017 Laureus Comeback of the Year Award
- 2016 Golden Google Impact Award
- Swimming World American Swimmer of the Year Award (2001, 2002, 2003, 2004, 2006, 2007, 2008, 2009, 2012, 2015, and 2016)
- Michael Phelps Foundation

His achievements are numerous, and he got all these as an ADHD patient. In spite of all of the symptoms of ADHD he exhibited as an athlete, he kept on chasing his dreams. This is just one out of many highly successful people in our world today who beat all odds and achieved their dreams. Don't forget that parents, their dreams, not someone else's. Now is the time to discover the dreams of your ADHD children and support them in being the best they can be.

ADHD may have its challenges but those challenges can be turned into strengths and serve a greater good. Your ADHD child can live a near-normal life if only you'll invest your time, attention, encouragement, and support in helping them physically, mentally, academically, and socially.

Parenting ADHD with Empathy And Effectiveness

Use the principles in this book to channel their energy to profitable things. Enlighten them about themselves and why they act the way they do. Go on to show them their strengths and weaknesses, but highlight the strengths. Tell them how to harness their weaknesses and make them strengths.

Teach them to use their superpowers of hyperfocus, problem-solving skills, creativity, wild imagination, and all that energy. Introduce helpful tools - fun activities, readjustments, modifications, and games - that will help improve their focus and social skills.

Teach them to set achievable goals, and it doesn't have to start big. Take baby steps, like ensuring they complete everything on their visual calendar for each day. Motivate them with reinforcements and rewards where necessary. See and applaud their good more than you correct their bad.

Tell them what you expect from them, not what you don't. Be more emphatic but positive while talking to them about an issue. You don't want to make them feel hurt but you also don't want to pamper them till they can't do anything for themselves. Teach them to stand up for themselves and apply the mature response, silence, when talked down on in school or elsewhere.

Be their confidant, playmate, parent, adviser, friend, and teacher. See all the good they can be and tell them that every day. Never let them sleep with a negative mindset about themselves. Apply CBT and teach them mindfulness techniques to have a positive mindset and a calm, peaceful mind. Let them know that it's what they think and believe about themselves that matters most.

Tell them your story, and show them how even neurotypicals struggle every day. Let them see their challenges as a different kind of challenge from what others are facing, and not as a curse. Create a mental image in their mind on all they can be and achieve in life if they can only put in a little effort every day.

But remember, they can succeed but it mustn't be academically. Encourage them to explore their passions and interests and celebrate every process and success. I hope you've found the answers you seek in this book. I

Conclusion

believe as you apply these principles and teach these habits to your kids, it'll help them become better persons. I also hope you've found new lenses in viewing your ADHD child and you can now see their superpowers.

Now, use the principles you've learnt in this book and make a success out of your child. Tell a friend about this book if you really enjoyed it and please leave a comment as well. Thank you!

References

Bradt, Steve. "Wandering Mind Not a Happy Mind." Harvard Gazette, Harvard Gazette, 11 Nov. 2010, news.harvard.edu/gazette/story/2010/11/wandering-mind-not-a-happy-mind/.

Drew, Chris, and PhD. "11 Surprising Homework Statistics, Facts & Data (2022)." *Helpfulprofessor.com*, 23 Jan. 2022, helpfulprofessor.com/homework-statistics-data/.

Buchtel, Kristin. "Redirect Notice." Www.google.com, 24 Aug. 2022, www.google.com/amp/s/noteworthyparenting.com/blog/2022/8/24/helping-children-to-discover-their-passion-and-their-purpose%3fformat=amp. Accessed 3 Oct. 2023.

Cassata, Cathy. "My Child Has ADHD. Should We Have an IEP or 504 Plan? - ADHD Online." Adhdonline.com, 24 Aug. 2022, adhdonline.com/articles/my-child-has-adhd-should-we-have-an-iep-or-504-plan/. Accessed 3 Oct. 2023

Loveless, Becton. "Bullying Epidemic: Facts, Statistics and Prevention." Educationcorner.com, 2010, www.educationcorner.com/bullying-facts-statistics-and-prevention.html.

Pattemore, Chantelle. "10 Ways to Build and Preserve Better Boundaries." Psych Central, 3 June 2021, psychcentral.com/lib/10-way-to-build-and-preserve-better-boundaries#types.

Pera, Gina. "Empathy and Mirror Neurons: Or, Monkey See, Monkey Yawn." ADHD Roller Coaster—Gina Pera, 25 Sept. 2009, adhdrollercoaster.org/tools-and-strategies/empathy-and-mirror-neurons-or-monkey-see-monkey-yawn-baby-see-baby-dance/.

Astenvald, Rebecka, et al. "Emotion Dysregulation in ADHD and Other Neurodevelopmental Conditions: A Co-Twin Control Study." *Child and Adolescent Psychiatry and Mental Health*, vol. 16, no. 1, 28 Nov. 2022, https://doi.org/10.1186/s13034-022-00528-0. Accessed 4 Dec. 2022.

References

Buzanko, Dr Caroline. "How to Manage Impulsive Behaviours in Kids with ADHD." Dr. Caroline Buzanko, 27 Sept. 2019, drcarolinebuzanko.com/how-to-manage-impulsive-behaviours-in-kids-with-adhd/. Accessed 3 Oct. 2023.

Cherry, Kendra. "What Is Cognitive Behavioral Therapy (CBT)?" Verywell Mind, 10 Aug. 2022, www.verywellmind.com/what-is-cognitive-behavior-therapy-2795747.

Feyoh, Michal. "11 Free Time Management Worksheet for Students & Adults." Develop Good Habits, 9 Aug. 2022, www.developgoodhabits.com/time-management-worksheets/.

Hoffman, Karen Sampson . "Green Time for ADHD." CHADD, 20 July 2023, chadd.org/adhd-news/adhd-news-caregivers/green-time-for-adhd/#:~:text=For%20children%20with%20ADHD%2C%20enjoying.

Lindberg, Sara. "Helping Your Child with ADHD Manage Screen Time." Healthline, 11 Feb. 2022, www.healthline.com/health/adhd/10-tips-for-helping-kids-with-adhd-manage-screen-time#tips. Accessed 18 Sept. 2023.

McQueen, Janie. "Childhood ADHD and Screen Time." WebMD, 28 May 2022, www.webmd.com/add-adhd/childhood-adhd/childhood-adhd-screen-time.

Pinnix, Karie. "ADHD Time Management 101: Tips for Being on Time." Www.getinflow.io, 25 Apr. 2023, www.getinflow.io/post/adhd-and-running-late. Accessed 3 Oct. 2023.

Preiato, Daniel. "ADHD and Exercise: What You Need to Know." Healthline, 19 Oct. 2021, www.healthline.com/health/fitness/adhd-and-exercise#exercise-and-adhd.

R, Denise. "The Importance of Goal Setting for Children." ChildWatch, 12 May 2019, childwatch.com/blog/2019/05/11/the-importance-of-goal-setting-for-children/.

Sippl, Amy. "Long-Term Self-Monitoring Strategies | Life Skills Advocate." Lifeskillsadvocate.com, 20 June 2023, lifeskillsadvocate.com/blog/self-monitoring-long-term-strategies-supports/.

Spector, Nicole. "What Is Self-Awareness? And How Can You Cultivate It?" NBC News, 9 Nov. 2019, www.google.com/amp/s/www.nbcnews.com/better/amp/ncna1067721.

Tripp, Gail. "Carrots vs. Sticks: The Science of Reward and Punishment for Children with ADHD." ADDitude, 9 May 2022, www.additudemag.com/positive-reinforcement-reward-and-punishment-adhd/#:~:text=It.

Victorino, RC. "The Eisenhower Matrix: Prioritize Your Time on What Matters Most - Knock down Silos." Slab.com, 23 Sept. 2020, slab.com/blog/eisenhower-matrix/.

Ahmad, Fatima, et al. "Healthy Meal, Happy Brain: How Diet Affects Brain Functioning." Frontiers for Young Minds, vol. 9, 3 Aug. 2021, kids.frontiersin.org/articles/10.3389/frym.2021.578214, https://doi.org/10.3389/frym.2021.578214.

Collingwood , Jane. "The Genetics of ADHD." Psych Central, 17 May 2016, psychcentral.com/lib/the-genetics-of-adhd#2.

Gillespie , Claire . "For Most Children, ADHD Continues into Adulthood, Study Finds." *Verywell Family*, 21 June 2023, www.verywellfamily.com/adhd-continues-into-adulthood-for-most-children-study-finds-5199788. Accessed 25 Sept. 2023.

Goally. "Adapting a Style of Communication with Your Child with ADHD." Goally Apps & Tablets for Kids, 13 June 2023, getgoally.com/blog/communication-with-your-child-with-adhd/#:~:text=Your%20ADHD%20Child-.

Kumperscak, Hojka Gregoric. ADHD through Different Developmental Stages. Www.intechopen.com, IntechOpen, 27 June 2013, www.intechopen.com/chapters/44753.

Narins, Elizabeth . "Active Listening: Tips to Engage with Your Child." Www.thebump.com, 28 Apr. 2023, www.thebump.com/a/active-listening. Accessed 3 Oct. 2023.

Shakibaie, Sarah. "Importance of ADHD Support Groups for Parents (and What to Expect)." Ready Kids, 4 May 2022, readykids.com.au/adhd-support-group/#:~:text=The%20Importance%20of%20Support%20Groups&text=support%20groups%20helpful%3F-. Accessed 3 Oct. 2023.

Wong, Cathy. "Mindfulness Meditation." Verywell Mind, Verywellmind, 8 Apr. 2021, www.verywellmind.com/mindfulness-meditation-88369.

www.ingramcontent.com/pod-product-compliance
Lightning Source LLC
Chambersburg PA
CBHW062225080426
42734CB00010B/2025